Sitting Bull

AND THE BATTLE OF THE LITTLE BIGHORN

Alvin Josephy's Biography Series of American Indians

Sitting Bull

AND THE BATTLE OF THE LITTLE BIGHORN

Written by Sheila Black

INTRODUCTION BY ALVIN M. JOSEPHY, JR.
ILLUSTRATED BY ED LEE

Silver Burdett Press

Project editors: Nancy Furstinger (Silver Burdett Press)
Mark Davies & Della Rowland (Kipling Press)
Designed by Mike Hortens

10 9 8 7 6 5 4 3 2 1 (Lib. ed.)
10 9 8 7 6 5 4 3 2 1 (Pbk. ed.)

Library of Congress Cataloging-in-Publication Data

Black, Sheila (Sheila Fiona)
Sitting Bull and the Battle of the Little Big Horn / by Sheila
Black ; introduction by Alvin M. Josephy, Jr.
p.   cm. — (Alvin Josephy's biography series of American
Indians)
Bibliography: p. 131
1. Sitting Bull, Chief of the Sioux, 1831-1890—Juvenile
literature. 2. Dakota Indians—Biography—Juvenile literature.
3. Hunkpapa Indians— Biography—Juvenile literature. 4. Little Big
Horn, Battle of the,—1876—Juvenile literature. 5. Indians of
North America—Great Plains—Biography—Juvenile literature.
I. Title. II. Series.
E99.D1S563   1989
970.00497—dc19
[B]   88-27021
CIP
AC
ISBN 0-382-09572-3 (lib. bdg.)   ISBN 0-382-09761-0 (pbk.)

Contents

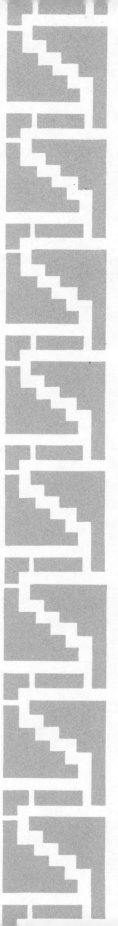

To the Sioux people
who continue to fight for their nation.
S. B.

Although this book is based on real events and real people, some dialogue, a few thoughts, and several local descriptions have been reconstructed to make the story more enjoyable. It does not, however, alter the basic truth of the story we are telling.

Unless otherwise indicated, the Indian designs used throughout this book are purely decorative, and do not signify a particular tribe or nation.

∞   ∞   ∞

Introduction

For 500 years, Christopher Columbus has been hailed as the "discoverer" of America. But Columbus only discovered America for his fellow Europeans, who did not know of its existence. America was really discovered more than 10,000 years before the time of Columbus by people who came across the Bering Strait from Siberia into Alaska. From there they spread south to populate both North and South America. By the time of Columbus, in fact, there were millions of descendants of the true discoverers of America living in all parts of the Western Hemisphere. They inhabited the territory from the northern shores of Alaska and Canada to the southern tip of South America. In what is now the United States, hundreds of tribes, large and small, covered the land from Maine and Florida to Puget Sound and California. Each tribe had a long and proud history of its own. America was hardly an "un-

CREE

BLACKFOOT

CANADA

NOOTKA

WA

CHINOOK

YAKIMA

FLATHEAD

TILLAMOOK

COLUMBIA RIVER

GROS VENTRE

HIDATSA

SIUSLAW

WALLA WALLA

NEZ PERCE

MT

ND

OR

ID

CROW

MANDAN

SIOUX

TOLOWA

SHASTA

SD

MISSOURI RIVER

YUROK

MAIDU

BANNOCK

WY

ARIKARA

POMO

WASHO

NV

CHEYENNE

PONCA

MIWOK

UT

NE

OMAHA

COSTANOA

YOKUTS

ARAPAHO

PAWNEE

SALINA

CA

PAIUTE

UTE

CO

KANSAS

KS

CAHUILLA

NAVAJO

MOJAVE

HOPI

ZUNI

NM

KIOWA

YUMA

AZ

PUEBLO

COMANCHE

OK

WITCHITA

PACIFIC

PIMA

APACHE

TX

OCEAN

MEXICO

TONKAWA

RIO GRANDE RIVER

Map of
Continental United States
American Indians

MAP BY JIM ROBINSON

OJIBWA
(CHIPPEWA)

ALGONQUIN

MICMAC

ME

Lake Superior

MENOMINEE

OTTAWA

MAHICAN

VT

NH

SAUX

Lake Michigan

Lake Huron

HURON

ST. LAWRENCE RIVER

WI

MI

HURON

MOHAWK

IROQUOIS

MA

MASSACHUSET

MN

FOX

WINNEBAGO

Lake Ontario

ONONDAGA

RI

WAMPANOAG

KICKAPOO

POTAWATOMI

Lake Erie

NEUTRAL

SENECA

CAYUGA

ONEIDA

NY

CT

NARRAGANSET

PEQUOT

IA

IOWA

IL

MIAMI

IN

ERIE

OH

SUSQUEHANNOCK

DELAWARE

PA

NJ

MD

DE

MOHICAN

ATLANTIC

MISSOURI

MO

SHAWNEE

OHIO RIVER

WV

VA

POWAHATAN

OCEAN

OSAGE

KY

TUSCARORA

QUAPAW

AR

CHICKASAW

TN

CHEROKEE

NC

CATAWBA

SC

MISSISSIPPI RIVER

MS

AL

CREEK

GA

TUNICA

CHOCTAW

YAMASEE

CADDO

LA

N

W   E

S

BILOXI

NATCHEZ

ATATKAPA

TIMUCUA

0   100   200   300   400   500

SCALE IN MILES

APALACHEE

FL

SEMINOLE

GULF OF MEXICO

IX

known world," an "unexplored wilderness"—except to the Europeans who gazed for the first time upon its forests and rivers, its prairies and mountains.

From the very beginning, the newcomers from Europe had many mistaken notions about the people whose ancestors had been living in America for centuries. At first Columbus thought he had reached the East Indies of Asia, and he called the people Indians. The name took hold and remains to this day. But there were more serious misconceptions that had a tragic effect on relations between the Indians and the Europeans. These misconceptions led to one of the greatest holocausts in world history. Indians were robbed of their possessions, their lands, and the lives of countless numbers of their people.

Most Europeans never really understood the thinking, beliefs, values, or religions of the Indians. The Indian way of life was so different from that of the Europeans, who had inherited thousands of years of diverse backgrounds, religions, and ways of thinking and acting. The Europeans looked down on the Indians as strange and different, and therefore inferior. They were ignorant in the way they treated the Indians. To the white people, the Indians were "savages" and "barbarians," who either had to change their ways and become completely like the Europeans or be destroyed.

At the same time, many Europeans came as conquerors. They wanted the Indians' lands and the resources of those lands— resources such as gold, silver, and furs. Their greed, their superior weapons, and their contempt for the Indians' "inferior" ways led to many wars. Of course the Indians fought back to protect the lives of their people, their lands, their religions, their freedoms, their very way of life. But the Europeans—and then their American descendants—assumed that the Indians were all fierce warriors who fought simply because they loved to fight. Only in recent years have we come to see the Indians as they really are—people who would fight when their lives and freedom were at stake. People who were fun-loving children, young lovers, mothers who cried for the safety and health of their families, fathers who did their best to provide food, wise old people who gave advice, religious leaders, philosophers, statesmen, artists, musicians, storytellers, makers of crafts. Yes, and scientists, engineers, and builders of cities as well. The Indian civilizations in Mexico and Peru were among the most advanced the world has ever known.

This book gets beneath the surface of the old, worn-out fables to tell a real story of the Indians—to help us understand how the Indians looked at the world. When we understand this, we can see not only what they did, but why they did it. Everything here is accurate history, and it is an exciting story. And it is told in such a way that we, the readers, can imagine ourselves back among the Indians of the past, identifying ourselves with their ways of life, beliefs, and destinies. Perhaps in the end we will be able to ask: What choices would we have had? How would we ourselves have responded and behaved?

Sitting Bull and the Sioux were among the greatest of all American Indians. This is true because they fought so long and so hard for their independence and for the possession of their lands on the Great Plains of the American West. But Sitting Bull was more than a warrior. He was a great, inspiring holy man and the main religious leader of his own tribe—the Hunkpapa Sioux—as well as one of the most respected spiritual men among all the western Sioux.

When we read about him in this book, we learn much more than simply about the Sioux as warrior Indians of the plains and about the battles, like the Little Bighorn, in which these braves fought. We see the Sioux as a feeling and caring people with a way of life worth fighting and dying for. And that is exactly what Sitting Bull and many of his fellow Sioux did. The story of their heroic struggles, their will to be free, and their tragic deaths is one of the greatest—and saddest—epics that the history of America has to tell.

—Alvin M. Josephy, Jr.

A buffalo skin, decorated with battle scenes

1
A Broken Promise

The Indians knew before anyone else.

On the afternoon of June 26, 1876, the Crow and Shoshoni Indian scouts in General George Crook's camp at Goose Creek, Wyoming, grew nervous, staring at the ground with wide, frightened eyes.

"What is it?" the general asked, for he knew his scouts well and could tell something was wrong.

The scouts refused to answer.

The general asked them again. But still the scouts would say nothing.

"For God's sake, *what is it?*" he asked them a third time.

At last they told him. There had been a big fight between the Indians and the American soldiers at the Little Bighorn River, farther north in Montana. Almost all the soldiers were dead.

General Crook was startled. He was one of the most experienced Indian fighters in the country. He had led a campaign against the Apaches in Arizona, and had learned more about Indian ways than had most white people. It was he who had taught his soldiers to travel light to keep up with the fast-moving, agile Indian warriors. The Crows trusted him so much that they had made him an honorary member of their Soldier Lodge, a club of warriors. General Crook thought nothing about Indian fighting could surprise him or make him lose his nerve. But there was something about what the scouts said that made his blood run cold.

Eagerly he pressed them for details. But they would tell him nothing further.

It was late afternoon. The sun was sinking slowly. The camp was full of the sounds of men carrying out their normal duties. Some were cleaning guns. Others were lighting fires and boiling water for the evening meal. Laughter and snatches of songs floated through the air. But despite all this activity, the general could not help feeling a little bit shaken. As the sun set, his small, alert eyes roved around restlessly as he gazed north in the direction of Montana.

What if the Indians were right? the general wondered. And if they were, how had they learned of the fight so quickly? Through smoke signals? Or through some other, even more mysterious way of talking to one another?

The general never learned the answer. But on July 10, fifteen days later, when an exhausted Army messenger at last reached the camp at Goose Creek, the general discovered that the story the Indian scouts had told him was true.

General George A. Custer, the famous Indian fighter—whom many of the Indians called "Long Hair" because of his flowing blond locks—had led the cavalry under his command in a march toward the valley of the Little Bighorn River. In this group were 636 men, 616 of whom belonged to the crackerjack Seventh Regiment—the cream of the U.S. Army's Indian-fighting troops. Once he reached the valley of the Little Bighorn, Custer had ordered 235 members of the Seventh Regiment to attack a large Indian camp on the banks of the river. Neither Custer nor any of his men had survived.

The Indian camp Custer attacked numbered about 12,000, with about 3,000 fighting men, or warriors. The camp was made up of a number of different tribes of Plains Indians. There were the Oglala Sioux, led by the legendary warrior Crazy Horse; the Cheyennes, who followed their ablest warriors, Two Moon, Lame White Man, and Charcoal Bear; and the Miniconjous, led by Chief Hump and Chief Lame Deer. Also present were the Sans Arc, Blackfeet, Two Kettle, and Brule Sioux, a few Arapahos, and even some eastern Yanktonai and Santee Sioux. Last but not least, there were the powerful Hunkpapa Sioux, led by their strong-willed chief and visionary medicine man Sitting Bull and their brave war chief Gall.

Afterwards, no one could figure out why Custer had attacked such an unusually large and diverse gathering of Plains Indians. But he was known to be reckless and hungry for glory. Besides he had never thought the Indians were particularly good at fighting.

On that distant day in 1876, however, he discovered his error.

Custer and 235 of his men were killed in about an hour by Indian warriors. Their bodies were left to lie bloody and broken in the ravines and on the slopes leading to the Little Bighorn River.

The only survivors of the Seventh Regiment were some of the soldiers who belonged to the six troops Custer had sent ahead. Three troops of 125 men, led by Captain Frederick Benteen, had been ordered to march south to scout for Indians. Two more troops had been ordered to give chase to some Indians who Custer spotted across the Little Bighorn River. These 112 men, under the command of Marcus A. Reno, had ended up attacking the south end of the big Indian camp. Joined later by Captain Benteen's forces, they had engaged in a long, desperate battle with the Sioux warriors. They had escaped with their lives only because the Indians had at last decided to give up the fight and move on. And so, Reno, Benteen, and their terrified men, unaware of what had become of General Custer, survived to tell the tale of what would later become known as the most famous battle of the West.

When the news reached the Goose Creek camp, General Crook immediately got his 2,000 men together and ordered them to pack up and begin marching north. His orders were to find and punish the "hostile" Indians responsible for Custer's death. In particular, he wanted to find the men who had led them—the Oglala Sioux warrior Crazy

Horse and, most important of all, Sitting Bull, leading chief of the
Hunkpapa Sioux.

By now news of Custer's shocking defeat had spread to the East.
All across the country, people were crying out for revenge against the
"bloodthirsty redskinned" savages who had killed the gallant General
Custer. Sitting Bull was condemned as a "coldblooded murderer." It was
he, the soldiers said, who had brought the Sioux and Cheyenne tribes
together to do battle with the American Army. It was he who was behind
the terrible massacre. And so as the days grew longer, and the midsummer sun blazed down on the hills and valleys of the vast Indian
country (which included large parts of the Dakota, Montana, and
Wyoming territories), a number of armies fanned out over the northern
plains to search for the proud and hostile chief.

Most of them gave up after a time. But General George Crook
continued his search, leading his men north—through the Dakota
Territory.

Meanwhile, people in cities as far apart as Boston, Massachusetts,
and St. Louis, Missouri, made solemn vows to seek out and kill Sitting
Bull and the other warrior chiefs in revenge for the death of their golden-
haired hero.

But in the general outcry, few Americans stopped to ask themselves
why General George A. Custer had attacked the large Indian camp on
the banks of the Little Bighorn River. Also, more importantly, no one
asked the next logical question: Why were Sitting Bull and his followers
fighting against the white people in the first place?

To most Americans at the time, the Indians of the plains were
barely more than savages—a little-known, picturesque people who lived
in the great wilderness miles and miles west of the Mississippi. And the
land that the Plains Indians were fighting for—a remote territory of
pine-covered hills and open, rolling plains—seemed almost as far away
as the moon. But that was not so for the Indians.

To the Sioux who had lived there for generations, this land—and
in particular the region known as the Black Hills of South Dakota—
was the center of the world. The Black Hills, which the Sioux called
Paha Sapa, were holy lands. In this wild country of green valleys and
lofty mountains, Sioux people of all ages went to purify themselves

and pray to their great creator spirit, Wakan Tanka, for visions that would answer their pleas. Here medicine men looked into the future and tried to understand the past. This untouched land was the soul of the Sioux nation. Here, buffalo and deer ran wild, berries grew, and clear streams flowed.

The Sioux had been promised that the Black Hills would be theirs for "as long as the grass shall grow and the waters flow." In 1868 the United States government had made this promise in a treaty signed by all seven Western Sioux tribes, along with some of the Eastern, or Dakota, Sioux. But a few years later gold had been discovered in the hills, and the United States government decided to take this rich country away from the Indians. First they offered to buy it. But when the Sioux refused to sell, the United States Congress declared it sold anyway. The Indians still living there in freedom were told to report immediately to government reservations where they would be watched over by government agents. No longer would the first Americans be able to move freely as they chose, or follow the way of life that they had always known.

The Black Hills

When government messengers brought this order to the Indians of the Black Hills, one middle-aged Sioux chief decided that the time had passed when his people would live in peace with the white people, or make any more arrangements with them. To preserve the land they loved, and to save their traditions and their freedom, the Sioux would have to fight.

The name of this chief was Tatanka Yotanka, or "Sitting Buffalo Bull." He was a leading medicine man and war leader of the Hunk-papas—a branch of the Western, or Lakota, Sioux. Although most Americans did not know his name until after the Battle of the Little Bighorn, his story began many years before then, at a time when the white people had not yet begun to move westward in great numbers, a time when the proud Sioux people were still the masters of the Great Plains of the northwestern part of the United States.

ᘰᘰᘰᘰᘰ *2* ᘰᘰᘰᘰᘰ

A Boy Named Slow

In the winter of 1831 on the snow-covered banks of Willow Creek, in the part of the country that is now South Dakota, a Hunkpapa Sioux warrior named Returns-Again and his wife, Mixed-Days, celebrated the birth of their first son.

The baby boy would grow up to become one of the most famous Indians of the plains: Sitting Bull. At first, however, the baby was given no name. It was the custom among the Sioux that a person must earn the name he or she would carry into adulthood. This was especially true of boys. The Sioux believed it was up to the young men to prove by their deeds that they were worthy to carry a good name, a name worthy of a warrior.

This is how the baby's father, Returns-Again, had earned his name. It was said that no matter how fierce his enemies were, or how badly he was hurt in battle, he always returned to fight again.

Returns-Again was strong and agile. A proud Sioux warrior, he could fire ten arrows from his bow before the first one had even reached its target. He could tame and ride the wildest of horses, and he was a wise hunter. Returns-Again was also a man of vision. Sometimes he had the gift of understanding the "speech" of animals. And on rare occasions, he could even look into the future. But one thing he could not see was what would become of his newborn son. And, at first, the boy worried him.

His son was large and slow-moving. Unlike other babies in the Indian camp, he did not try to grab at things or turn himself over. Instead he kept still, studying everything around him with wide, serious-looking eyes. When Returns-Again tried to make the child smile or laugh, the baby merely stared at him without so much as a flicker of recognition. And when he did do things, he appeared clumsy and awkward.

Before long everyone in camp had named the child Hunknesi, or "Slow." Returns-Again grew even more worried. Perhaps his son was slow in the head. But his wife, Mixed-Days, had no such worries. Her son, she said, was not the least bit stupid. She showed her husband how carefully the boy observed everything around him and how well he remembered what he saw. The baby might be clumsy, but he was certainly intelligent. He was only slow because he was cautious, careful, even stubborn. And before long, others noticed this about the baby, too.

"Unlike most children," one Hunkpapa said later, "Slow would not just grab a piece of food and put it in his mouth. Instead he would turn it over in his hands, studying it. But once he decided he wanted it, you could not get it away from him."

In his own quiet way, Slow was busy watching and learning about the world around him.

It was a strange, exciting place.

Slow's people, the Hunkpapa Sioux, were one of the most powerful tribes in the area. They were hunters and warriors. In pursuit of game, they moved from place to place across the territory then known to the white people as the Great American Desert. To the white people, this was a harsh country of tough grass, barren, rocky hills, and mountains that could not be crossed—a land the American writer Washington Irving said was "as vast and as untracked as the ocean." But Slow's people did not think of it that way at all.

The Hunkpapa Sioux had not always lived in this vast, little-known part of America. Long ago they had been a forest tribe in the East. But battles with the more powerful Chippewas, who had been given guns by the white fur traders, had forced them West.

Buffalo

The land they had wandered into was sparsely populated, even by Indians. And to the Sioux, it was as if they were the first people ever to come there. Huge herds of buffalo roamed across its grassy plains—so many that their hoofbeats made a sound like thunder. At first, the Sioux moved through this new land on foot. But they soon got horses from tribes farther to the south, who in turn had gotten them from the Spanish settlers to the south of them. Little by little the Sioux became expert horsemen. Like other tribes of the area, they also became skilled at stealing horses from their enemies. On horseback, hunting and moving from place to place became much easier. So did fighting the other tribes who lived in this wild country that the Sioux now considered their own.

But even with horses, it was not an easy land in which to survive. In winter the plains grew so cold that a person could freeze to death only a few steps from camp. There were terrible blizzards and whiteouts, in which the entire world seemed to be swallowed up in a cloud of icy snow. And in summer the sun blazed down like a fierce eye, until the entire landscape grew parched and barren.

To prosper in this country, Slow's people had become tough—fierce, proud, and warlike. Yet they were also a mystical people. The land the Sioux now lived in was unspoiled and beautiful, and they paid great attention to it. They believed their god, the Great Spirit, Wakan Tanka, lived in the endless blue sky above the plains. To get close to him, the Sioux studied everything in nature, convinced that the Great Spirit was present in each of them. They learned the ways of the animals of the earth and the sky. To the Sioux these animals were like members of their family, to be respected and honored. And of all the animals of the earth—the "four legs," as the Sioux called them—the most important was the buffalo.

The buffalo gave Slow's people everything they needed to live. Its meat fed them. From its skins they made the robes they wore and the coverings for the tepees that housed them. Its hooves gave them glue, and its horns were used to make cups and tools. From its sinews, they made thread for their needles and strings for their bows. Even their movements from camp to camp had to do with where the great herds of buffalo roamed. For without the buffalo the Sioux could not hope to survive.

As a tiny child, Slow soon came to understand how important the buffalo was to his people's way of life.

As soon as he was old enough to talk, he heard hunters sing songs honoring the great furry creature of the plains. He watched the braves go out on buffalo hunts, returning several days later with freshly killed buffalo meat. At such times the entire camp would celebrate. And for many days all the Indians would feast on roasted buffalo ribs and tasty stews. Slow often watched his mother scrape buffalo hides to make a new covering for their tepee or new robes for himself and his father. He learned how buffalo meat could be sliced and dried as jerky to be eaten later. He saw how it was pounded and mixed with fat and berries to make a food called pemmican. This was stuffed into intestines to be eaten later also. But, most of all, he learned how his people moved about endlessly as they followed the path of the buffalo.

At such times, Slow's mother would take down the family tepee. Then she would load all their possessions on his father's sturdy ponies or on the travois, a kind of sled made of two long poles and light branches of wood that the horses dragged behind them across the prairie.

Slow always enjoyed these journeys. When he was a small child, he traveled with his mother on her big bay horse. But by the time he was eight, he had learned to ride by himself. And that year, his father gave him a pony of his own.

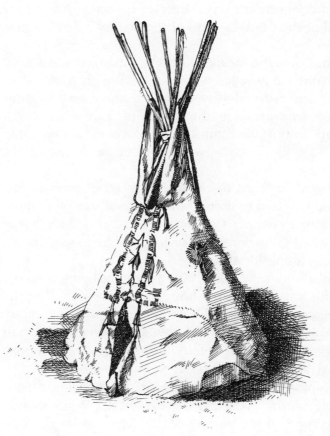

Sioux tipi

It was a small gray pony, and Slow loved it with all his heart. He pretended the little pony was as fast as a bolt of lightning and that he was a great hunter like his father—or, better still, a brave and fearless warrior.

Slow had often seen his father go out with the other warriors to fight the Crows or the Blackfeet, tribes that were enemies of the Sioux. His father and the others would dress themselves very carefully for these battles. The braves painted their faces to resemble eagles or fierce grizzly bears. They wore magic charms to protect them from harm. And on their heads they placed bonnets of eagle and hawk feathers, often dyed all different colors. When they returned from a victory—often with captives and horses that they had taken from their enemies—the entire camp would celebrate for days. Everyone would gather to listen to the warriors tell of their bravery and of the "coups" they had taken against their enemies.

A "coup" was the greatest honor a warrior could achieve. It meant that he had touched his enemy alive or dead with a special stick called a "coup stick" and escaped alive. It took a brave man to come that close to a fierce enemy warrior, and to touch or tag one's enemy in this way was far more important than killing or injuring him. Only men who had taken "coup" in battle were allowed to boast of their bravery afterwards.

Slow loved to listen to the warriors tell of their coups. Over and over again he repeated to himself their tales of hard-fought victories and of daring raids in which the warriors escaped with herds of enemy horses. His heart grew fierce and proud, and he longed for the day when he would fight alongside them.

But for a long time, Slow only played at being a warrior with the other boys his age, using a toy bow and arrow his father had made for him. He began to wonder if he would ever grow big enough to go to battle. He was fourteen years old now and tired of being only a boy.

One warm night as he stared moodily into the campfire, a warrior named Good-Voiced Elk called out to him in a low voice.

Good-Voiced Elk said that tomorrow morning a war party was going out against the Crows. Slow's eyes lit up. When Good-Voiced Elk saw the eagerness in the boy's face, be began to laugh. Slow must not get any ideas, he said. This was no job for boys. Then, as suddenly as he

12

had spoken, he slipped away into the darkness.

Slow stared into the fire. Then he made a decision. When the war party left, he would be with them.

It was summer and the sky was thick with stars.

That night, Slow lay in his mother's tent with his eyes wide open. He was afraid to fall asleep in case he might sleep too late and miss the war party.

The camp was silent except for the whispering of the grass. A warm wind stirred up the dust around the flaps of the tepee. Slow tossed and turned. At last his eyes closed.

When he woke up, the light was gray and pale. The boy leaped to his feet and dashed out to where his little gray pony was tied up. Quickly, he mounted the pony and rode silently to the edge of camp. He had no weapon, but he did have a coup stick his father had made for him. It was red—the sacred color—the color of all good things. Holding it carefully before him, Slow rode out to meet the warriors.

They were all ready to go. A line of them stood before him on horseback in full war paint. With serious eyes they stared as Slow made his way toward them. He could see his father right in the center. His face was stern.

Slow sat up as straight as he could. He clung tightly to his pony, feeling as if it were his only friend in the world.

"We are coming, too," he announced in a small but steady voice.

The warriors began to smile, even his father. Then they began to speak among themselves. It seemed to take a very long time.

At last his father looked up at him and nodded. He could come with them!

In a single graceful movement, the line of Sioux warriors swung around their horses and set out across the plain. They were going to a place named Red Water, where some Crows had been spotted. Clicking his heels, Slow urged his little pony to gallop faster and faster, until, like the others, he was swept up in a cloud of dust.

They rode for a long time. The sun rose and the sky became a piercing blue. The ground grew hot and bright. At last Good-Voiced Elk made a signal to Slow to be quiet. The Crows were just over the next hill.

The boy's heart thumped hard in his chest. When something was

13

good or strong, the Sioux said it was "cha," or red. Later Slow said that his heart felt very "red" that day. Before he knew what he was doing, he found himself dashing over the hill, his little gray pony charging even faster than the big horses of the other warriors. He was chanting a war song and lifting his coup stick high in the air.

The other Sioux urged their horses after him, but the boy was already over the hill.

The Crow warrior on the other side could hardly believe his eyes. The Sioux coming toward him was only a boy, and he did not even have a real weapon. The Crow warrior raised his bow and fitted an arrow to it. But before he could fire—bam! Slow struck him on the arm with his coup stick, and the bow fell from the Crow's hand.

The other Sioux warriors quickly fell upon him, and within minutes the Crow lay dead.

When the other Crows saw how quickly their fellow brave had been killed, they fled over the hills, leaving horses and provisions behind them.

The Sioux burst into a song. It had been a good day. But the greatest honor of the battle belonged to Slow, for it was he who had taken the first coup against the enemy.

The boy was brave.

In triumph, the war party made its way back to camp. Returns-Again rode at the head of the Sioux warriors with his son beside him. He was proud and wanted everyone to know what the boy had done.

In the family tepee, he painted the boy from head to toe with the black color of victory. Then, placing him on one of his finest horses, he led him slowly around the Hunkpapas' camp while everyone looked on.

"My son is brave!" Returns-Again chanted. "He is brave. From this day on, he will be called Sitting Bull!"

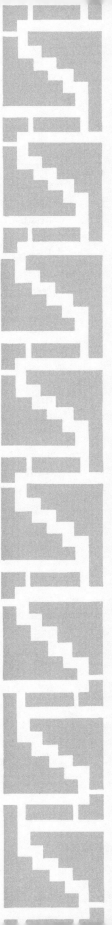

3
Slow Earns a New Name

Sitting Bull, or Tatanka Yotanka, was a magic name. As a boy, Slow had often heard his father tell the story of how he had first heard it. Many years ago, when Slow was only a small baby, Returns-Again had gone on a hunting trip with two other men. Because it was summer, they slept out in the open. One night, as they were about to go to sleep, they heard someone approaching their camp. Returns-Again leaped to his feet. In open country, enemy attack was always a danger.

Stepping as lightly as he could, Returns-Again peered through the tall grass. His companions did the same. Soon they saw that the intruder was not a man but a giant buffalo. Swaying slowly from side to side, the huge animal came toward them. Returns-Again could hear it muttering to itself, and when he listened closely, he found that he could understand what it was saying: "Sitting Bull, Jumping Bull, Bull with Cow, Bull All Alone." Over and over again, the giant buffalo repeated this phrase. Then, at last, it turned and lumbered off into the darkness.

The other two Hunkpapas had not been able to understand what the buffalo was saying. But when Returns-Again told them, their eyes grew wide. Returns-Again had received a message from the Great Spirit, a mark of good fortune. The buffalo's words described the four ages of life: childhood, youth, maturity, and old age. Four was the sacred number of the Sioux. It was said that all good things came in fours: the seasons of the earth and the ages of man. The Great Spirit had given Returns-Again a gift of four names. Like the giant buffalo, a symbol for all that was young and strong and wise, these four names would bring strength and wisdom to whomever carried them.

At first Returns-Again kept the first and most powerful of these names for himself. But when he gave this name—Sitting Bull—to his son, he took for his own the second name—Jumping Bull.

The name Sitting Bull would belong only to Slow.

The games Slow had played as a child were put aside when he got his new name. Now Sitting Bull entered in earnest the life of a Sioux man—a Sioux warrior.

The Sioux took great pride in their warriors and in their reputation as a fierce, proud people. One of their favorite stories told how once, many years before, a group of Sioux warriors were out hunting when they came across a group of Iroquois.

"What are you looking for?" the Iroquois asked them.

"We are looking for buffalo," the Sioux replied. "What are *you* looking for?"

"We are looking for men!" the Iroquois answered.

"Well," said the Sioux, "We are men. You need look no further!"

Upon this a great battle broke out, and the fighting was so fierce that a huge cloud of dust rose up over the plain. When the dust settled at last, the Sioux were all standing, but almost all of the Iroquois were dead. The ones that were still living begged the Sioux to spare them. This, the Sioux did, saying: "Go! But tell your chiefs to send no more *women* looking for *men*!"

The young Sitting Bull often listened to this story and others like it. He could not imagine a more noble life than that of a warrior, fighting to win glory for his people. Like the other young braves, he eagerly offered to join the war parties that went out against the Crows, the Blackfeet, and other enemy tribes.

The Sioux had fought with the other Indians of the plains for as long as anyone could remember. They had some friends— above all, the Cheyenne. But they had more enemies, and the greatest of these were the Crows. The Hunkpapas often went out to attack the Crows and to steal their horses. All the best horses came from the south, where the Crows lived. And for as long as there had been Sioux on the plains, they had depended on these fleet Crow horses to carry them. The Crows, in

Running fight: Sioux and Crow

17

return, often attacked the Hunkpapas. They usually came in the middle of the night or at the break of dawn, when everyone was asleep. Then they would fill the air with their blood-curdling cries. As far as the Sioux were concerned, however, the Crows were no match for them. *Their* warriors were the strongest and bravest of all.

It was not easy to be a Sioux warrior. It required courage, skill, and endurance.

Like all young braves, Sitting Bull had learned how to string his bow in the blink of an eye. He had learned to unleash his arrows with such force that they would go through anything, even the thick, leathery hide of a buffalo. He had learned to use a knife, a tomahawk, and a hatchet, and how to ride straight at the enemy without flinching.

Often in the gray light of dawn, Sitting Bull and the other Hunkpapa warriors set out on raids against their enemies. Silently they would slip into sleeping camps, rounding up horses and ponies as fast as they could. Then they would escape over the hills, with their enemies in hot pursuit. Often, too, Sitting Bull and the others faced off against lines of Crow or Blackfeet warriors, all brave and ready to die. He had enjoyed great victories, and had tasted defeat. He had seen friends and relatives cut down in the prime of life by enemy arrows. And sometimes he had even felt afraid. At such times he had repeated an old Sioux proverb to give himself courage:

> *It is better to die naked on the plain*
> *than to rot on the scaffold.*

Old men and those who died in sickness were laid out on high scaffolds of wood so that their souls might rise more easily to the land of the Great Spirit. But the greatest honor for a warrior was to die in battle. A truly brave man should not expect to live forever.

Yet, although Sitting Bull was brave, he was not reckless as some young warriors were. He was still too "slow" for that. He liked to think things out—to make a plan before he acted. This made him especially useful when the Hunkpapas went out to steal horses. No one could decide better than he the best time to strike at an enemy camp. No one could round up ponies more smoothly. Before long, he was, as one writer of history said, "perhaps the ablest horse thief this country has ever produced."

18

And this talent for making plans made Sitting Bull a powerful hunter as well. He was skilled at tracking and trapping all the animals of the earth—buffalo, deer, elk, and antelope. He learned where the animals went in different seasons, how to imitate their characteristic sounds so that they would approach without fear, and how to kill them quickly and painlessly.

His name was a magic name, and so, as a young man, Sitting Bull also studied the wisdom of the medicine men of his tribe. He learned from them the ways of the Great Spirit—how to smoke the sacred pipe of peace and how to carry out the rituals sacred to his people. He learned that the Great Spirit is within all things of the world—grass and mountains, fish and birds. Yet it is also above all things. And a good man must never neglect to honor the Great Spirit. Whenever Sitting Bull killed an animal, he always thanked the Great Spirit, as he had been taught. Then he offered up part of the meat, with these words:

> *Grandfather, the Great Spirit behold me!*
> *To all the wild things that eat flesh,*
> *This I have offered,*
> *That my people may live and the children*
> *Grow up with plenty.*

In this way, the young Sitting Bull believed, the spirit world paid him back so that he and his people would always be cared for and protected.

Like his father, Sitting Bull found that he could sometimes understand the "speech" of animals. When he was an old man, he often told of the first time this had happened.

One day, when he was seventeen, he fell asleep by the bank of a creek. It was a hot day, and before long he was sleeping very deeply. He began to dream. In his dream a huge, fierce grizzly bear came toward him. Soon it was standing over him with its paws raised. Suddenly a little bird—a yellow jackdaw— appeared beside him. "Wake up, Sitting Bull! Wake up!" the small bird sang. Sitting Bull opened his eyes and found that his dream had come true. There was a grizzly crouched over him, ready to attack! Sitting Bull was about to get up and run when suddenly he heard the yellow jackdaw beside him, just as in his dream. The little jackdaw began to sing, and to his amazement he could understand all that it said.

19

"Do not be afraid!" the bird sang. "But keep still, keep still. If you do not move, the bear will not harm you."

Sitting Bull did as the little bird told him. Sure enough, after a while, the bear fell back on all fours and, grunting to itself, loped off into the woods.

To thank the little yellow bird for saving his life, Sitting Bull composed a song:

> *Pretty Bird, you saw me*
> *And took pity on me*
> *You wish me to survive*
> *Among the people*
> *Oh bird people from this day on*
> *You shall be my relatives.*

Sitting Bull often made up such songs. He did so not only to celebrate magic things but also to describe the ordinary day-to-day life of his people. He made up songs about good hunts and victories in battle, songs that poked fun at foolish people and praised wise ones, songs of love, and songs of worship. Whenever he made up a new song, the other Hunkpapas gathered to listen. And his special talent soon made him one of the most popular of all the young warriors.

4 "All Things Pass"

Sitting Bull was now old enough to be married. Hunkpapa men were allowed to take more than one wife, and in his lifetime, Sitting Bull had many. But his first was a girl he had known since he was a young boy.

Her name was Scarlett Woman. She was beautiful and gentle, with long, shining braids and large, deep eyes. Sitting Bull felt as if he had always loved her. So, now that he was old enough, he gave her father a gift of many fine horses and asked permission to make her his wife.

Scarlett Woman's father agreed, and the young couple soon moved into a tepee of their own, made of fine buffalo leather bleached white by the sun. The following year Scarlett Woman gave birth to a baby boy.

It was a happy time for Sitting Bull.

Now, when he returned from hunting or from hard battles, his wife and baby were waiting for him. And when summer came Sitting Bull and his wife spent many pleasant hours walking together beside cool creeks or playing with their infant son. Unlike his father, the baby was a lively little fellow—always squirming about like a small fish, always laughing and smiling.

Sitting Bull considered himself a lucky man. But then the winter came.

It was a hard winter—colder than usual, with blinding snows and bitter frosts. With the cold weather came sickness, and before the first thaw of spring both his young wife and his newborn son were dead.

Sitting Bull moved back into his mother's tepee. But although Mixed-Days did what she could to comfort him, for a long time nothing would console Sitting Bull. He could not forget Scarlett Woman or his little son. Spring came, then summer, but Sitting Bull barely noticed. The world had lost its sweetness.

Sioux baby-carrier

Then, little by little, the sorrow began to ease. He remembered what he had been taught by wise men as a child: "Nothing on this earth lasts forever. All things pass. He who knows this knows that he is nothing compared with Wakan Tanka who is everything; then he knows that world which is real."

These thoughts helped to heal his pain. Once more he began to find pleasure in living.

It was winter again—a dull, sad time. Men and women stayed close to camp, gathering around fires and telling stories. Sitting Bull was eager for action, but nothing much was happening. Then one day a warrior named No-Neck came to see him. He and some other braves were going out on a horse-stealing raid against the Crows. Would Sitting Bull come, too?

Sitting Bull agreed eagerly. He did not much like No-Neck—a grumpy, bearlike man who was known for his bad temper—but the sun was shining bright on the snow. It was a good day for a fight.

Off they sped on their horses, looking for the Crow camp which was said to be nearby. But, although the Hunkpapa warriors rode for a long time, the Crows were nowhere to be found.

They were about to give up when No-Neck, who had gone up ahead, shouted that he had found an Assiniboine tepee pitched beside a small stream. It looked as if there would be a fight after all!

Like the Crows and the Blackfeet, the Assiniboine were old enemies of the Hunkpapas. But, unlike the others, the Assiniboine were not very good warriors. In fact, the Hunkpapas never failed to beat them. "This poor tribe cannot take care of itself," the Hunkpapas used to say. "They are forever getting themselves killed." This day was no different.

The Assiniboine tepee contained a single family—a father, a mother, a newborn baby, a boy of about five, and an older boy of about eleven. They were no match for No-Neck and his friends. Within minutes, they all lay dead—all except the eleven-year-old boy.

All alone, he faced the fierce Hunkpapa warriors. But he was a brave child and did not cry or try to run. Instead he stood right up to them, raising his toy bow and arrow before him.

Sitting Bull, who had lagged behind the others, now came riding up. Something about the child's courage touched him. Seeing Sitting Bull's gentle expression, the little boy cried out: "Big Brother, help me!"

23

Sitting Bull could not understand what the child was saying, but quickly he dismounted from his horse and moved beside the little Assiniboine.

"Leave him alone!" he ordered No-Neck and the others.

No-Neck began to grumble. The boy was his prize. He had found him, and he could kill him if he chose to.

But Sitting Bull stood firm. He wished to adopt the boy as his little brother, he said. And if any of them harmed the child in any way, they would have *him* to answer to. All the warriors except No-Neck fell back. They knew what a strong warrior Sitting Bull was, and they did not want trouble.

No-Neck, however, kept on insisting that the boy was his, and he would argue his case before the entire tribe.

Silently the group made its way back to camp, and with Sitting Bull rode the Assiniboine child.

In camp No-Neck proclaimed loudly that Sitting Bull had robbed him. He insisted that the Assiniboine boy by rights should be his to kill. Was it not strange, he asked, that Sitting Bull should wish to take an enemy into his own family?

The other Hunkpapas were confused. It was an odd thing to do, they agreed, but Sitting Bull was a good and wise man. He must have his reasons.

At last Sitting Bull came forward to explain himself. He told of the courage of the Assiniboine child and of how the boy had asked for his help. When he was done, he succeeded in making all the other Hunkpapas feel sorry for the boy, who had lost his whole family. Sitting Bull said nothing about it, but the members of the tribe could tell that he was thinking of Scarlett Woman and the son he had lost the winter before. At last they decided that Sitting Bull could adopt the boy if he chose.

And so the Assiniboine became Sitting Bull's little brother.

At first the Hunkpapas called him Stays-Back. They chose the name because, even though Sitting Bull told him he could return to his own people if he chose, the boy decided to remain with the Hunkpapas.

When he grew up, however, the boy was given a new name. He was called Kills-Often, for in battle he was almost as brave as Sitting Bull himself. He never failed to bring harm to his enemies. From then on, 1857—the year Sitting Bull adopted the boy—was known in the Hunkpapas' calendar as "The Year Kills-Often Came to Stay."

No-Neck never forgave Sitting Bull for stealing his prize. But in later years the other Hunkpapas said that Sitting Bull showed great wisdom in sparing the life of the brave Assiniboine. What he had done, they said, showed that he had the heart not only of a great warrior but also of a great man.

The same year that he brought home Kills-Often, Sitting Bull received a great honor. He was elected to the greatest of all the Hunkpapa warrior societies: the Strong Hearts. The Strong Hearts were so-named because their hearts never grew weak at the sight of their enemies. They were brave men who did not retreat from a fight. The Strong Hearts had a special lodge of their own where they often gathered to sing songs of war and to tell of the coups they had won. The Strong Hearts had many special songs that only they were allowed to sing. Sitting Bull soon wrote some new ones. One of these annoyed his mother so much that she begged him *never* to sing it in her presence. It went:

> *No chance for me to live, Mother*
> *You might as well mourn!*

Whenever Sitting Bull sang it, his mother accused him of being heartless and of not caring about her. But Sitting Bull only laughed. It was just a song to give the warriors courage. Besides, he had been to battle many times and he had never yet been hurt. Didn't his mother want him to be a brave man?

Mixed-Days *did*, but she simply could not become accustomed to that song. The other Strong Hearts loved it, however, and often asked Sitting Bull to ride at their head, singing it as loudly as he could. Although he was still a young man, he was one of their leading members. He could always be counted on to rally the warriors and never to retreat without making sure his other Strong Heart brothers were safe. Because he was so loyal, he was soon elected to the most honorable position in the Strong Hearts. His title was sash wearer.

A group of Sioux Indians

The sash wearer of the Strong Hearts wore a special costume when he went to battle. He was given a beautiful bonnet of buffalo horn and black crow feathers. From this trailed a long, thin sash of red cloth that ran all the way to the ground. In battle the sash wearer pinned this sash to the ground with his lance. This showed that he would not retreat until his enemies had been beaten, or until one of his own warriors unpinned him.

In the old days, when this custom first started, the Sioux fought on foot. So a sash wearer stood a good chance of surviving. Facing enemy on horseback this way, however, was another matter. A man pinned to the ground was an easy target for an enemy on a horse. Now it took a brave man indeed to be a sash wearer, and many chosen for the honor

26

did not live long to enjoy it. But Sitting Bull not only survived, he wasn't even hurt. The Great Spirit must be watching over him, the other Hunkpapas said. And their admiration for him grew.

His father was especially proud of him. Returns-Again was an old man now, and often he stayed up late into the night and told his son tales of old times—when people still remembered how the Sioux had first moved into the West. Sitting Bull must be sure to remember these tales, for his father would not be alive to tell them much longer, the old man cautioned.

Sitting Bull tried to tell his father he would live for many years, but old Returns-Again would have none of it. He wanted to die, he said. He was ashamed that he had grown so old and weak. "I am no good for anything anymore," he said. And it was true that each day he seemed to grow weaker.

One day Returns-Again came down with a terrible toothache. The pain was so sharp that all day and night he moaned. "I only wish to die," he cried over and over, "to die like a man."

The next morning, Sitting Bull left camp with the other young men of the tribe to go hunting. While the young men were away, a party of Crow warriors attacked. The Hunkpapas were not prepared, and soon several members of the tribe lay dead.

Inside the ring of tepees a Crow chieftain, stronger and fiercer than the rest, paraded back and forth. On his head was a great bonnet of eagle feathers, and in his hand was a gleaming new rifle. None of the Hunkpapas dared approach him, not with their best warriors gone. And so the mighty Crow chief rode back and forth, daring someone to come and fight him.

But no one did.

Then old Returns-Again rose from his bed. Peering through the flaps of his tepee, he saw the Crow chief. He could not believe that no one was challenging him. How dare this Crow showoff parade himself among the Hunkpapas in this way! Returns-Again decided that he, as old as he was, would go out against him. Mixed-Days begged him not to do anything so foolish. But Returns-Again shook her off, saying: "Last night I had a terrible toothache and wished I was dead. Now my chance has come and I have longed for such a day."

Paying no attention to his wife's tears, the old man dressed himself for battle. Carefully he painted his face red for victory. Then, taking his bow and arrows, he fetched his favorite horse.

Returns-Again could no longer see as clearly as he once had, and the years had streaked his hair with gray, but now he sat up strong and tall and rode straight toward the fierce Crow chief.

The Crow was not at all frightened to see Returns-Again come toward him. Lifting his rifle, he fired it at the old man, hitting him once in the side and once in the arm. But old Returns-Again just kept riding toward him.

The Crow chief fired again, striking the bow from the old man's hand. But Returns-Again still did not give up. He pulled out his knife and kept advancing. He was now close enough to the Crow warrior to reach out and touch him with his coup stick, but he was losing blood quickly. He lifted his knife to strike, but it slipped from his fingers and fell to the ground. The Crow chief pulled out his knife. Stabbing down hard, he pierced old Returns-Again straight through the skull.

With a slow sigh, Returns-Again slid from his horse and fell to the ground dead.

A great wailing broke out among the Hunkpapas, and Mixed-Days ran over to her husband's body.

But still none of the Hunkpapas dared fight the mighty Crow chief, who turned and rode away from the camp.

Shortly afterwards, Sitting Bull and the others returned from hunting. When Sitting Bull saw his father's body, he began to wail so loudly that the camp shook with his cries. When he heard what had happened, Sitting Bull grew angry. His eyes blazing, he scolded the Hunkpapas. How could they let the Crow chief go without trying to get even for his father's death? Were they all cowards?

A murmur welled up from the warriors who had been out hunting. They could not let the death of Returns-Again go unpunished. One and all, they mounted their horses. Then, like angry hornets, they swarmed out after the Crows who had attacked their camp.

They galloped over the hills so fast that a cloud of dust rose around them. Before long they caught sight of the Crows. Sitting Bull quickly spotted the tall, mighty warrior who had murdered his father. Spurring his horse forward, he raced after him. The Crow tried to escape, but

Sitting Bull was too swift. His lance raised, he bore down on the Crow and with a single blow knocked him from his horse. Then he drew out his knife and within minutes the mighty Crow lay dead.

He had avenged the death of his father.

With a great holler, the other Hunkpapas charged in pursuit of the remaining Crows. They were hungry to fight, because Returns-Again had been much loved by all the Hunkpapas. For thirty miles they rode across the prairie until the sun rose high and bright. Then they reached the sharp ridge of Rainy Butte, which cut into the sky like a great knife.

Here they at last caught up with the Crows. As one, the Hunkpapas attacked. They fought so recklessly that the Crows soon fled in terror, leaving three women and a baby boy behind them. The Hunkpapa warriors took the women and children captive and headed back to camp.

Sitting Bull rode behind them. He was sad and quiet, his hair loosened in mourning. He had taken his revenge, but his father was still gone. He had not even said goodbye to him.

The other warriors soon arrived back at camp with the Crow captives. The Hunkpapas gathered to meet them. They all felt sorry for Sitting Bull. They knew how much he had loved his father and how angry he was about his murder. By rights the captives should be his to kill if he wished—in revenge for his father's death. The Hunkpapas looked over the Crow women and the child and talked over what should be done. But not even his friends and relatives could agree.

Some said that it was only right that he should be allowed to take revenge for his father's death. The captives were his to do with as he chose. But others felt sorry for them. These captives were women, not warriors. It was not fair that they should die. At last everyone agreed that the best thing would be to hide the captives for a while. When Sitting Bull had grown calm again, they would give them to him. Perhaps then he would no longer wish for revenge.

When Sitting Bull returned to camp, he could see by his friends' faces that something was wrong. He had seen the other warriors take captives, and now the captives were nowhere to be found. He puzzled over this for a while. Then he understood. Drying his eyes, he said to the Hunkpapas: "If you have hidden the captives for my sake, it is not right. I will not take their lives. Treat them well and let them live. My father was a man, and death is his." With this, he turned and walked away from the camp. As he walked, he thought of his father and remembered all that he had learned from him.

It was indeed true, as his father and other wise men had told him, that all passes away like smoke from a fire. Because of this, life was both hard and sweet, for in this world things you loved were always being lost or changed forever.

But he comforted himself with the thought that some things did not change. There was always the buffalo, the grass, and the sky. There was always the Great Spirit who guarded the sacred way of his people, which never changed, and, like a circle, went on forever. And as long as these things were there, life would be good.

But far east of the Lakotas' country, events were occurring that would change forever these things that Sitting Bull believed to be permanent.

The white people were moving west.

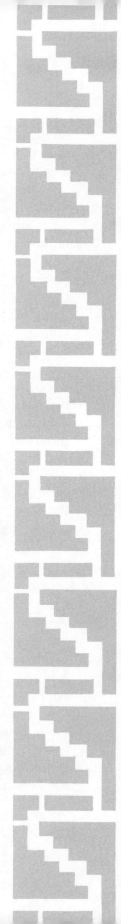

5
Moving West

When Sitting Bull was a boy, he saw few white people, or Wasichus, as the Hunkpapas called them. Aside from the occasional trapper or trader, white people almost never traveled that far west. Most of what the Hunkpapas knew of this strange tribe to the east came from stories others had told them. They knew the white people were powerful. They had seen their guns, which seemed to work almost by magic. But the Hunkpapas did not waste too much time thinking about them. To them the Wasichus were simply a strange people from a faraway place—something to be curious about and not much more.

The land where Sitting Bull's people lived was called "Permanent Indian Country." By 1840 its border ran from eastern Minnesota down across Missouri and Arkansas to the edge of Texas. At the time, the American government was willing to let the Indians keep this land forever. As far as they were concerned, it was worthless—a harsh land that no one wanted or needed. Nothing, it was said, would grow on the vast grassy plains where the buffalo roamed. White people would never be able to live there. It was a wasteland that led nowhere.

But over the next ten years, this vision of Indian Country changed rapidly.

America was growing rapidly. By 1840 there were about twenty million American citizens, and more people were coming every year. From Europe and Asia, men and women poured into the United States, drawn by the promise of making a better life for themselves and their children. In this vast, untamed country, it was said that any man could make his fortune. There were plenty of jobs, and miles of land for the taking.

But the East, where most Americans lived, was getting crowded. New York, Boston, and Philadelphia were now big, bustling cities. They were filled with large office buildings and huge, noisy factories. Competition was fierce. The streets teemed with men hustling for jobs. Apartment houses and row houses were thrown up to shelter the thousands of new immigrant workers. Even the countryside in the East was no longer open. Most of it had been settled a long time ago. America's reputation as the land of easy opportunity was fast becoming a thing of the past. Many Americans began to turn a longing eye to the West, where the world was still empty and there was land enough for all.

In 1842 an adventurous group of Americans set out on a long journey that would one day mean the end of Permanent Indian Country. These were the settlers who opened up the Oregon Trail, which led westward to the rich lands along the Pacific Ocean.

Eighteen wagons carrying a hundred settlers set out from Independence, Kansas. Their route took them northwest across present-day Kansas, Nebraska, and Wyoming, right through the heart of Indian country—and finally into the Oregon Territory.

Probably the Indians hardly noticed their passing. After all, the first Oregon settlers were such a small party. But once the route had been set by these first settlers, many more would follow.

Other events also were changing the attitude of America toward the Permanent Indian Country.

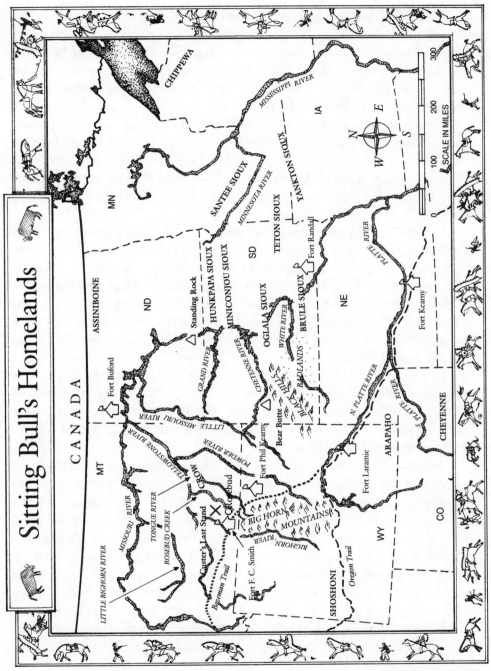

Sitting Bull's Homelands

MAP BY JIM ROBINSON

In 1845 Texas became the twenty-eighth state of the Union. The following year the entire Oregon Territory also became an official part of the United States. Even more importantly, in 1848, President James K. Polk signed a treaty ending the Mexican War. This treaty extended the Southwest of the United States all the way to the Pacific Ocean, giving America the rich California Territory.

To Americans everywhere, the West was rapidly becoming more important and more attractive. Suddenly, the land of the Plains Indians was no longer a barren desert leading nowhere. Now it was becoming a vital passageway to new American lands—lands that many Americans were eager to explore and settle in. And each year the movement west grew.

In 1847 the Mormons grew tired of being persecuted for their religious beliefs. They decided they would try their luck out west. Moving westward from Council Bluffs, Iowa, they joined the Oregon Trail near Fort Kearny in Nebraska. They then traveled parallel to the Oregon Trail along the north side of the Platte River, moving across central Nebraska through central and southwestern Wyoming. But even the number of Mormons moving west was nothing compared to what came two years later.

In 1848 gold was discovered in California. The following spring, a huge parade of gold prospectors, nicknamed the "forty-niners," poured down the Mormon and Oregon trails. Wagons stretched as far as the eye could see as people, eager to make their fortunes, made their way to the promised land of California.

The Indians of the plains no longer had their country to themselves.

Along the trails, the ground became littered with tin cans, pieces of clothing, and carcasses. The loud guns and creaking wagons of the settlers scared away the buffalo, elk, and antelope that had once been plentiful there. To the Indians these white people were a nuisance— but they were only passing through. Indeed, most of them showed no interest in staying longer than was absolutely necessary. To these white people, Indian country was still a frightening, mysterious place. They wanted to cross it as quickly as possible and then leave it far, far behind.

But now the United States government took a new interest in the Permanent Indian Country. More and more of their citizens were passing through it every year, and their safety needed to be ensured. The

Gold prospectors

U.S. government could no longer afford to leave the Indians alone. It was time to make a new treaty.

In 1851 government messengers were dispatched to all the Indians of the plains, asking them to come to a meeting at the newly built Fort Laramie along the Oregon Trail.

The meeting took place at the end of the summer. It was the largest gathering ever of the Plains Indians. All the tribes came—the seven great bands of Western Sioux, the Cheyenne, the Arapahos, the Crows, the Shoshonis, and many others. Tepees stretched like a forest of trees and everywhere Indians greeted old friends. At this point, they were curious to hear what the white people would tell them.

The council lasted for twenty days. At last a treaty was agreed upon.

In this treaty, signed by all the chiefs, the Indians promised not to harm settlers passing on the Oregon Trail. They also agreed to allow the United States government to build forts to protect the trail. In return for allowing the white people to enter their land, the Indians were to be paid fifty thousand dollars for fifty years, mostly in the form of food and other useful supplies.

After the treaty was signed, the tribes packed up and moved away. Most of the chiefs were pleased with the bargain they had made. But it was not long before they came to see that what it really meant was trouble—trouble for them and their people.

Soon the terms of that treaty were being changed.

First the United States Congress said that fifty thousand dollars multiplied by fifty years was far too much money to give a bunch of "wild Indians." Instead they would give them fifty thousand dollars for five years. When they heard of this, the chiefs grew angry. But it was not long before they had even more serious problems to worry about.

They had given the white people permission to *pass through* their land. But the white people translated this to mean that they could treat the land as their own.

More travelers came down the trails each year. With their rifles, they disturbed the ancient peace of the country. They shot the buffalo in great numbers, killing them not just for meat, but for sport. Before long, the buffalo began to keep well away from the trails. The travelers killed other animals as well, and it was not long before game became scarce. The Indians began to go hungry in their own land. Yet every year more settlers came and with them came more soldiers.

Forts had been built all across the Indian country. Often, when the Indians approached these forts, the soldiers would begin firing at them for no reason. Now, whenever the Indians had a dispute with the settlers, the soldiers came too. No matter what had happened, they acted as if the Indians were to blame.

The Plains Indians were being treated like outlaws in their own country.

In 1854 a war was almost started when a Mormon settler accused a young Brule Sioux of stealing one of his cows. The Brule claimed that he had found the cow wandering lost. Being hungry, he had killed and eaten it. He had not stolen it. But the white people refused to listen. At last the Brule chief, Conquering Bear, hurried to Fort Laramie and offered to pay for the cow. But the soldiers demanded a price that was much too high, and Conquering Bear said he could not pay it. He left for home again. The next day, however, the Army sent out thirty men under the command of Lieutenant Grattan to force the Indians to make amends.

The young, bold Lieutenant Grattan liked nothing better than an excuse to fight some Indians. He did not try to discuss the matter peacefully with Conquering Bear and his people. Instead Grattan approached with guns and cannons. In a loud voice, he demanded that the young man who had killed the cow surrender immediately. When the Indians argued, he opened fire, killing several Brules instantly and so badly wounding Conquering Bear that he died a short while later.

Shocked and frightened, Conquering Bear's people rose up and attacked the soldiers. Within a few minutes, Grattan and all his men lay dead.

When the U.S. Army learned this, they decided to punish the Indians for what had happened.

The following year an army of 1,500 men, under the command of Colonel William Harney, was sent out to take revenge for the slaughter of Grattan and his men. Full of fiery words, they marched out along the Platte River until they came across a band of Sioux under the leadership of Chief Little Thunder.

Little Thunder's people had nothing to do with the stolen cow or the death of Grattan and his men. But that did not matter to the soldiers. Harney's men immediately opened fire on the unarmed camp. Within moments Little Thunder and most of his people had been killed.

The policy of the white people was clear. If any Indian did anything, *all* the Indians were to blame and would be punished.

After Colonel Harney's brutal attack, an uneasy peace settled over the plains. But it was only a resting period. The time of real peace between the Indians and the white people was gone.

The next tribe to suffer was the Santee Sioux—Sitting Bull's relatives.

⌦⌦⌦⌦⌦ **6** ⌦⌦⌦⌦⌦

"Let Them Eat Grass"

The Santees were Eastern, or Dakota, Sioux. Their chief was named Little Crow. They lived in the beautiful country of Minnesota, a country that was not all prairie but broken up by shady woods and clear lakes. For some time settlers had been coming to this rich land, which was good for farming. The Santees had worked hard to make peace with these settlers. By 1862, however, they found that they had not received much in return for their efforts to make peace with the white people. The Santees were now all living on a reservation ten miles wide and one hundred and fifty miles long. It was a poor trade for the hundreds and hundreds of miles of rich land the white people had tricked and bullied them into giving up.

In return for the loss of their land, the Santees had been promised yearly payments of food, supplies, and money. In 1862, however, these payments were late in coming.

Abraham Lincoln

The Civil War was being fought. Northern and Southern states were in the middle of a bitter struggle that would decide the fate of the Union.

The war had come about over the issue of slavery. The South held slaves, and believed they needed slave labor to operate their vast cotton plantations. In the North, however, slavery was not legal, and many people believed it should not exist at all. As new territories were added to the United States, the debate grew more bitter. The North insisted that slavery was wrong and should not be allowed in these new lands. The South, on the other hand, was just as eager to see slavery spread. Neither side could reach an agreement.

In 1860, when Abraham Lincoln was elected president, this quarrel flared into open warfare. Lincoln belonged to the new Republican party, which most Southerners believed would soon put a stop to slavery altogether. Rather than see this happen, the South decided it would break from the Union and form a country of its own. In April 1861,

Southern troops attacked Fort Sumter, South Carolina, driving the U.S. Army forces out. When Lincoln heard of it, he declared war.

Now, two years later, the American government was putting all its resources into fighting the Civil War. Money was needed for troops and supplies. And far away in Minnesota, this meant that the payments promised to Little Crow and his people were being delivered later and later.

In order to be present when payment arrived, the Santees had put off going on their annual buffalo hunt. Now they were starving, but still the promised food and supplies did not come.

At last, Little Crow went to see Thomas Galbraith, the reservation agent, to plead for his people. When he arrived at the agency headquarters on the Yellow Medicine River, he begged the agent to give the Santees food from the agency warehouses, which were filled with flour, pork, and dried corn. But Galbraith said he could not give them food until the money that was due them arrived.

Little Crow begged him to think it over. His people were starving. They needed the food *now*. Galbraith hesitated, then he turned to the traders, who had gathered to listen to the discussion. "What would you do?" he said. Andrew Myrick, one of the wealthiest traders, stared at Little Crow and spoke insolently. "If they are hungry, let them eat grass," he said.

And so Little Crow was sent away with his hands empty. But the Santees' anger was growing—and two days later it exploded.

On that day, August 17, four young Santee braves went out hunting. But they failed to catch anything. Feeling hungry and bad-tempered, they decided to return to camp. On the way, one of them found a nest of hen's eggs. He was about to take the eggs. But then another brave said the eggs belonged to the white people, and if he stole them, there would surely be trouble. The first brave accused the second of being a coward. "You are afraid of the white people!" he cried angrily, for he was very hungry and wanted to eat the eggs. The second said he was not. Slowly the argument between them got worse, until the first brave challenged the others to kill some white people to prove they were not cowards.

The young braves did not really want to do this, but no Sioux could allow himself to be called a coward. And so, with their hearts beating wildly, they made their way to a nearby settler's house. There they killed the three men and two women they found inside.

When they looked around at what they had done, the young braves became afraid. They rushed back to the camp to tell the other Santees what had happened.

When the young braves told their story, a great hush fell over the Santee camp.

The Santees knew enough about white people to know that they would surely all be punished for the crimes these young men had committed. From this moment on, none of them would be safe.

Many of the warriors argued that it was time for the Santees to fight. The white people would probably come and kill them anyway. Besides, the Santees had much to be angry about. Their land had been stolen. The payments they had been promised had not come. They were poor and hungry. It was time to give the white people some of their own medicine.

But Little Crow disagreed. Unlike the young warriors, he had traveled to the East and had seen the great cities there where the white people lived in huge numbers. He knew his people could not hope to beat the white people. There were too many of them, and they were much too powerful. "Braves," he cried, "you are little children—you are fools. You will die like rabbits, when the hungry wolves hunt them."

But the Santees would not listen. They cried out that Little Crow was a coward. He was afraid to fight.

Little Crow looked at them a long time. At last, he said: "Little Crow is not a coward; he will die with you."

And so it was that Little Crow, who wanted only peace, led his people to war.

First the Santees attacked the agency where they had been refused food. In a rage, they killed twenty men and took ten women as prisoners. The remaining forty-seven settlers at the fort managed to escape. Then the Santees set fire to all the buildings and looted all the warehouses. Among the dead they left at the agency was the trader Andrew Myrick—his mouth stuffed with prairie grass.

After their attack on the agency, the Santees believed they had nothing to lose. They fought furiously and showed their enemies no mercy. As they moved down the Minnesota Valley they attacked all the settlers they found—killing many and taking even more prisoner. They were headed for Fort Ridgely, twenty-five miles away on the banks of the Minnesota River. This fort guarded the entire southwestern part of the state. If Little Crow and his people could take it, they would have control over much of the Minnesota Valley.

On August 20 they made their first attack on the fort, early in the morning. But the soldiers' artillery managed to hold back the attack. When nightfall came, Little Crow and his warriors had made no progress, and so they retreated back to their camp. The next day it rained. Many more warriors came from the north to join Little Crow's forces; almost the entire Santee nation had come together at the camp on the Minnesota River. The following morning they would try to attack the fort again.

This time the attack started much better. The Santee warriors shot flaming arrows into the fort and soon set fire to several of the buildings. But the soldiers did not panic: with the help of some of the settlers and fierce artillery fire, they once again managed to force the Indians to withdraw.

When the Santees failed to take Fort Ridgely, Little Crow decided that perhaps he and his warriors could bypass the fort by marching down the south bank of the Minnesota River. To do this, however, Little Crow and his men first had to capture the village of New Ulm twenty miles downstream. This would eliminate the risk of attack from the rear and give the Santees a base from which to launch an attack on the settlers in the lower valley.

Early the next morning, the attack on New Ulm began. Out of the sunlit woods streamed a great arc of Sioux warriors heading straight toward the village. But when they got there, the Santees found the citizens of New Ulm were ready for them.

Barricades had been set up, and every man held a weapon. The women and children had taken shelter. Although Little Crow's warriors fought long and hard, they could not win a clear-cut victory. The settlers were too strong for them. At last Little Crow's warriors gave up the fight and retreated up the valley.

The Santee warriors had failed to capture Fort Ridgely or New Ulm—the all-important keys to the lower Minnesota Valley. Tired and disheartened, they moved back north to the reservation.

Soon they learned that an army of 1,400 men was approaching them from St. Paul, to the east. At their head was a man well known to the Santees—General Henry H. "Long Trader" Sibley.

Sibley had been the first governor of Minnesota and before that he had been a fur trader for many years. The company that he worked for, The American Fur Company, had bought many furs from the Santees. When the treaty that was supposed to pay the Santees for their land was signed, Sibley claimed, on behalf of the company, that the Santees had charged him too much for these furs. He demanded and won a third of their treaty money. The Santees felt Long Trader Sibley had robbed them. They knew him to be a hard-headed, cold-blooded man. And they were afraid of what he would do to them with an army behind him.

Soon after Little Crow and his men had moved north again, Sibley and his troops arrived at Fort Ridgely. For three days, Sibley sent his men out around the fort searching for Little Crow's warriors. When he found none, he sent one hundred and sixty men toward the lower agency to search for the bodies of settlers killed in the fighting. Sibley's men moved cautiously northward, burying the dead settlers they found. On their second night, Sibley's advance party decided to make camp at Birch Coolee, a deep ravine on the north side of the Minnesota River. That night Little Crow's men, who had seen the soldiers approaching, surrounded the camp and attacked. Many of the soldiers were killed and the battle only ended thirty-one hours later when Sibley at last arrived with the rest of his troops to rescue his hard-pressed men.

During early September the Santees and the soldiers engaged in many skirmishes. Little Crow's people fought bravely, but no matter how hard they struggled, Sibley's army proved too strong for them.

Many of the Santees were now eager for peace. They saw that they could not hope for any real victory, and wanted only to save what they could. They were tired and very much afraid. Alexander Ramsey, governor of Minnesota, had announced: "The Sioux must be exterminated, or forever driven beyond the borders of this state." The Santees wondered what would become of them.

With this in mind, Little Crow set about trying to make peace. On September 12, he sent a message to Long Trader Sibley. He informed him that the Santees had many prisoners, but were treating them kindly. If the general would agree to make a peace settlement, the prisoners would be released, unharmed. "I want to know from you as a friend," Little Crow wrote, "what way I can best make peace for my people."

Sibley's only reply was a cold demand that Little Crow let all his prisoners go and surrender immediately.

When Little Crow received Sibley's message, he knew all hope was lost. The white people were going to punish the Santees as harshly as possible. Little Crow's people had only two choices: death or exile.

And so Little Crow decided to lead his people west into the Dakota Territory, leaving behind forever the rich and pleasant land they had always known.

But not all the Santees agreed to flee.

On September 26, as Little Crow and his followers crossed the border into the Dakota Territory, 2,000 of the Santees who had remained behind surrendered to General Sibley, giving up 107 white and 162 half-breed prisoners.

These Santees had no desire to leave the land where they had been born. They hoped that as soon as the white soldiers realized they meant no further harm, they would be allowed to return to their reservation. But they soon discovered that the white people were not about to let them go so easily.

Of the 2,000 Santees who surrendered, 303 were sentenced to death for their "crimes." The remaining 1,700—mostly women and children—were taken to a prison camp 125 miles down the Minnesota River. In May 1863 these captives learned that they were to leave Minnesota forever. The white people were shipping them to a new reservation in the Dakota Territory.

Their new home was a small and barren patch of land on the banks of Crow Creek off the Missouri River. The soil there was not suited to farming and there were not many trees. The weather was harsh—cold and stormy in the winters, blazing hot in the summers. There was little food and the Santees soon began to starve. Before long, the hillsides of the new Santee reservation were dotted with graves. Of the 1,300 Santees who were taken to the reservation on Crow Creek, less than half survived the first winter.

In the spring of 1864, many of the other Sioux came to visit their unhappy Santee relatives. One of these visitors was Sitting Bull. What he saw at Crow Creek changed him forever.

The Santees had once been like his people—proud, cheerful, full of energy and courage. But now they were slow-moving and their eyes were dull. They did not seem to care whether they lived or died. Many told Sitting Bull stories of their war with the white people. They told how their land had been taken, and how the promises that had been made to them were broken. They told of how they had grown angry and decided to fight. It had all been for nothing, they said. Many said they wished only that they had been killed in their own country—to be buried in the good earth where they had been born and had once been happy. The Santees told Sitting Bull that the white people were like grasshoppers. They destroyed everything. They took everything. Soon there would be nothing left.

Sitting Bull listened. And when he saw how the Santees had suffered, his heart grew heavy. Then he made a vow: If the white people came for his country, he would fight.

Sioux medicine shield

45

A Rain of Bullets

After his visit to the Santees, Sitting Bull returned west. By the midsummer of 1864 he and the other Hunkpapas were camped on the Little Missouri River beside the mountain they called Where-They-Killed-the-Deer.

It was a pleasant spot, with fresh water, tall grass, and fragrant pine trees. Before long other bands of Sioux joined the Hunkpapas. Among them was a small band of Santees who had fled from Minnesota in 1862.

The camp was a busy, cheerful place. Friends and relatives who had not seen each other for a long time traded news and gossip. Women gathered spicy chokeberries and wild plums while children played games and swam in the clear river water. Each morning parties of young men went out hunting, and there was enough fresh meat for everyone.

But one morning a group of young men came rushing back to camp. Soldiers were coming! They had seen them over the hills, the buttons on their uniforms flashing in the distance like little suns.

The Sioux camp quickly moved into the hills.

Although Sitting Bull's people and the other western tribes considered themselves to be at peace with the white people, they had learned that it was better to be careful. You could never tell what a group of white soldiers might do when they found a band of Indians.

Mounting their horses, Sitting Bull and the other Hunkpapa warriors raced over the hills to take a look at the soldiers. Soon they spotted them. From the top of a high hill, they looked down at the long line of soldiers who were marching straight toward the camp.

Lone Dog, a Hunkpapa medicine man, announced that he would ride down and find out what the soldiers wanted. Lone Dog had made much strong magic in his time. Now he cried that even if the soldiers fired at him, he would not be hurt. He had a ghost who guarded him in battle. This ghost would keep even the white people's bullets from touching him.

Spurring his horse, Lone Dog galloped down the hill. As soon as he was in sight of the soldiers, they raised their rifles and began shooting. Bullets whizzed through the air, thick as rain. Later the Hunkpapas said that if Lone Dog's ghost had not been working hard that day, he surely would have died. As it was, he was forced to dodge this way and that. He was frightened and out of breath. But at last he reached the safety of the hilltop.

There could be no doubt about it. The soldiers meant war.

Sitting Bull and his warriors did not know it, but these soldiers had been marching toward them for some time. That spring they had been sent out as part of an army of 3,000 men under the command of General Alfred Sully. Their orders were to find and punish the Santees for what had happened in Minnesota two years before. It did not make any difference that Sitting Bull and his people had nothing to do with the events in Minnesota. The U.S. Army wanted revenge, and all Indians were a fair target.

As the soldiers drew nearer, more warriors gathered at the top of the hill.

Now, they decided, it was time to attack.

Shouting war whoops, the warriors sped off down the hillside, straight toward the line of soldiers. Showing their skill on horseback, the warriors zigzagged this way and that, avoiding the bullets that came at them from all sides.

But no matter how bravely they charged, they could not break the soldiers' line of formation. Whenever they came close enough to cause any damage, the soldiers all fired their guns fast and furiously, driving the Indian warriors back again.

Sitting Bull and the others had never seen so many guns, or guns that fired so quickly. Fighting the soldiers, they told each other, was not like fighting the Crows.

When they found that they were not able to advance against the endless rain of gunfire, the Indians decided to return to camp.

If they could not drive the U.S. Army soldiers, also known as bluecoats, back, they knew that they must at least delay them long enough to give the women and children time to escape.

As fast as they could, the warriors rode back to the foothills of Where-They-Killed-the-Deer Mountain. As they reached the camp a strange sight met their eyes. From the large ring of tepees came a cream-colored horse, dragging two travois poles and a basket made of willow branches.

In the basket sat a Hunkpapa they all knew well. His name was The-Man-Who-Never-Walked. He had been a cripple since birth. His legs were shriveled and useless. Nevertheless, he was painted for battle. And as he approached, Sitting Bull and the others could hear that he was singing a war song.

When he reached the line of warriors, The-Man-Who-Never-Walked announced that he was going to charge the bluecoats and kill as many of them as he could, before they reached the camp. The other warriors tried to stop him. But The-Man-Who-Never-Walked refused to listen. "I have often wished to defend my people in battle," he cried. "Today is a good day to die!"

As Sitting Bull and the other warriors watched breathlessly, he urged his horse forward, downhill toward the advancing soldiers.

As soon as the soldiers saw the cream-colored horse and the basket behind it, they began firing. Bullets hissed through the tall grass. Within a few moments, the horse fell, throwing the Man-Who-Never-Walked out of the travois basket. He sat facing the soldiers and singing his death song until the troops killed him.

The soldiers soon came marching up the hill. Meanwhile, the warriors formed a tight circle around the deserted camp. When the soldiers attacked, the Indians held their ground firmly, giving the women and children time to escape into the hills. The courage of The-Man-Who-Never-Walked had given them all heart and they fought hard to defend their people.

When sunset came, however, the warriors saw that it was impossible to hold the soldiers back much longer. There were too many of them scattered all over the side of the mountain. In the shadows of dusk, the Sioux warriors vanished uphill into the mountain. There they found high perches behind sheltering rocks and pine trees. They looked down at the soldiers who remained close by, guarding the empty camp.

When morning came, Sitting Bull and the other warriors were still awake, watching.

Soon many soldiers came marching into the camp. Some of the Hunkpapas decided to march down and meet them. They hoped that they could save all the tepees and possessions they had left behind. Fetching a piece of white cloth, they tied it to a stick of pine. Then, holding the "peace flag" high, they made their way down the hillside. The colonel who was leading the soldiers into the camp paid no attention to the flag the Indians were holding. Instead he shouted at his men to open fire. Once again the bullets came flying, and the Indians had to race back up the mountain.

From their hiding places among the still pines and ancient rocks, they watched as the bluecoats set fire to the camp. Soon all the tepees were burning. Buffalo robes and moccasins, children's toys and sacred charms all vanished in one long plume of smoke. When the bluecoats had finished burning the camp, they turned their torches to the grasses and pine trees that grew on the mountainside. Soon the woods were full of crackling flames.

Sitting Bull watched as the fire spread, consuming everything in its path. His mouth became a thin, hard line. The Santees were right. The white people destroyed everything.

For a long time he stared down at the soldiers. Then, joining the other Hunkpapas, he made his way swiftly over the hills.

Now Sitting Bull was eager to fight the soldiers again. Next time he and his warriors would win.

A few weeks later a message came from the Sans Arcs. They had been with the Hunkpapas at the camp at Where-They-Killed-the-Deer Mountain. Now they were fighting the soldiers again, this time at the crossing of the Little Missouri River in the country the white people called the Badlands. They wanted the Hunkpapas' help.

Sitting Bull and the others raced off to join the fight.

When they got there, they found two thousand soldiers stationed along the twisted trails that led through the canyons and ravines of the Badlands country. The Sans Arcs had fought hard at the crossing of the Little Missouri River. The soldiers were moving forward through the Badlands, trying to reach the Yellowstone River. But the Indians kept close to them and, this time, the Indians had the upper hand.

The soldiers were running out of supplies. At the Yellowstone River fresh supplies were waiting for them, but they had to get there first. Many of the soldiers were half-dead from hunger. Worse still, they could find little water fit to drink in the harsh, dry Badlands country. Their horses were dying under them.

The Indians, however, were doing fine. Sitting Bull and the other Sioux were accustomed to living in this fierce, dry country. They knew how to take care of themselves. With each passing day, the Sioux grew more and more confident.

The soldiers had wanted a fight, and now they were going to get one. Although the soldiers fought hard, the Indians did all they could to make the soldiers' progress as difficult as possible. The soldiers were rapidly losing heart.

One day, late in the afternoon, Sitting Bull and the others were surprised to hear voices calling to them in their own language from the soldiers' side.

"Help us!" the voices cried. "We are starving. The soldiers are dying, and there is no food here!"

The voices belonged to some Yankton or Eastern Sioux who had joined the soldiers as guides. Now they begged the Hunkpapas to take them in and save them. But Sitting Bull refused.

"Why have you come with these soldiers?" he shouted angrily. "The Indians here want no fight with white people. Why is it the whites come to fight with us, anyhow?"

Sitting Bull and the others waited for an answer, but the guides had nothing more to say.

Sitting Bull was tired of fighting. Many of his warriors had been wounded. They also were beginning to run low on food. "Come on," he said to the others. "Let's go home." The fight against the bluecoats had gone on long enough. It was time to forget war and go back to hunting.

When Sully's soldiers saw the Sioux ride away, they could not believe it. The Indians had been making it harder and harder for them to continue their long march. Why should the Sioux quit when they had the upper hand?

These soldiers did not understand the way of the Sioux. To a Sioux warrior the only good reasons to fight were to win glory or to defend one's people. They loved the art of battle—the quick daring of one-to-one combat. Slow, long, drawn-out battles like this one went against everything the Sioux warriors held dear. Now that the soldiers were leaving their land, there was no need to continue the fight. It was time to move on.

But if the soldiers were puzzled by the Indian's way of fighting, the Indians found the white people's war just as strange. Sitting Bull said of it later:

> *"The white soldiers do not know how to fight. They are not lively enough. They stand still and run straight. They do not try to save themselves. Also, they seem to have no hearts. When an Indian gets killed, the other Indians feel sorry and cry, and sometimes stop fighting. But when a white soldier gets killed, nobody cries, nobody cares; they go right on shooting and let him lie there."*

Sitting Bull did not like what he had seen of the white people's war. There was no honor in it. You could not fight man to man, or take coups on your enemy. It was just shooting and more shooting. But even so, he felt the time for peace had passed. The white people were rushing into his land, raising rifles against his people. If the bluecoats came back, he must work to defend his nation in any way he could.

Sitting Bull remembered something that had happened years before. Once, when he was a young warrior, he had gone walking in the sacred country of the Black Hills. High among the rocks, he had heard a man's voice singing a song he had never heard before. Climbing as high as he could into the hills, he looked for the singer everywhere. But he found no one. He was puzzled, and about to give up, when he looked up into the sky. There he saw a huge eagle, circling in the endless blue.

Wanbli Geleska

He knew then that the song he had heard must be the eagle's song. Wanbli Geleska, as the Sioux called the spotted eagle, could fly higher than any other creature. Of all living beings, it was the closest to the Great Spirit. Somehow the Great Spirit must have chosen Sitting Bull to hear this song—the song of the eagle—and take it to his heart.

Now, to give himself courage, Sitting Bull sang again the song he had heard the eagle sing so many years before in the sacred hills of Paha Sapa:

> *My Father has given me this nation*
> *In protecting them I have a hard time*

For the first time, he felt he understood all that the song meant. War was coming—war against the strange and powerful white people. He, Sitting Bull, must do all he could to defend his people against this new enemy.

8

The Powder River Invasion

Sitting Bull's mind was on war. But by 1865 many of the Hunkpapas were talking of peace. General Sully had retreated to Fort Rice, back east on the Missouri River. After his terrible experience with Sioux warriors in the Badlands country, Sully had no taste for fighting them anymore. "I feel sure I could defend myself if they attacked the fort," he wrote to the generals in Washington, D.C., "but that is about all I could do." As summer came, he sent messengers out to the Hunkpapa camp, asking them to come in and talk about a settlement.

The Hunkpapas discussed his message for a long time. Many felt they should go to the fort. The white soldiers were a powerful enemy. If the Hunkpapas fought them, there would be war for many years. It might be better to make peace. But others were not so sure, and among them was Sitting Bull.

"The white people have too many chiefs," he told his people. Even if one said he wanted peace, another might decide to go out and fight some Indians. Even if a treaty was signed, it could not be trusted. And he reminded the Hunkpapas of what had happened to their friends the Cheyenne, who lived to the south in the Rocky Mountain country.

The Cheyennes, under their kindly chief Black Kettle, had done all they could to live in peace with the white people.

It had not been easy. In 1858 gold was discovered in the Rocky Mountains. From all over the country miners came pouring into Cheyenne land. Many were rough, hard-boiled men—eager to make trouble. These newcomers also scared away all the wild game, making it hard for the Cheyenne to survive. Nevertheless, Black Kettle tried to persuade his people to follow the way of peace. Often he soothed angry young braves and warlike soldiers, offering the sacred pipe of peace to one and all. And Black Kettle kept the way of peace even after his people were driven from the mountains to a barren reservation on the sandy plains between Sand Creek and the Arkansas River.

On November 26, 1864, however, Black Kettle learned that all his efforts to make peace with the white people had been for nothing.

That morning, just before dawn, his camp at Sand Creek was awakened by the sound of gunfire. An army of white soldiers was coming toward them. Black Kettle rushed from his tepee and lifted high an American flag to show that his people did not want to fight. But the soldiers paid no attention.

The army of 750 men was led by Colonel Chivington. He had just arrived in Cheyenne country, and he did not care that Black Kettle and his people had always been peaceful. He believed it was his job to kill Indians. He also believed it was right to "use any means under God's heaven" to do it. An enormous man with a fat face, he preached a gospel of hatred to anyone who would listen.

The soldiers with him were drunk. Fired up by their colonel's speeches, they streamed into Black Kettle's camp. Their guns were raised and their bayonets were drawn. Chivington had ordered them to kill every last member of the camp, even the women and children. "Nits," he told his men, "make lice."

Among the first to die was one of the oldest members of the tribe— White Antelope, chief and medicine man. Walking straight toward his killers, White Antelope sang the death song of the proud Cheyenne:

Nothing lives long
Only the earth and the mountains

White Antelope might have been singing for all his people. By the time Chivington's men were done, most of the camp had been cut down, including about 110 women and children. The drunk soldiers had cut up their bodies in the most horrible way imaginable, hacking off limbs and gashing faces.

Black Kettle managed to escape with a handful of others. But no longer would the Cheyenne be at peace with the newcomers.

When Sitting Bull finished telling again the story of the massacre at Sand Creek, he turned on the Hunkpapas angrily. The Cheyenne had now promised to fight the white soldiers to the death. How could the Hunkpapas not choose to be with them? How could they trust the white people after they had done such a thing? War would come whether they wanted it or not. The Cheyenne, under their new chief Roman Nose, were even now battling the white soldiers to the south. Did the Hunk-papas imagine the white people would not make war on them, too? Peace was not possible.

With long faces, the other Hunkpapas agreed. And, at least in the beginning, events proved that Sitting Bull was right.

No sooner had Sully's "peace messengers" been sent on their way than a new army came marching into the Dakota Territory. These troops had ridden out from the newly built Fort Connor on the banks of the Powder River.

This army was in three columns. The first, under the command of General Patrick Connor, headed northwest along the Bozeman Trail, crossing the upper Powder. Connor's column then turned northeast along the Tongue River, before doubling back to march southwest along the Tongue. Along the Powder and the Rosebud, Connor's men had orders to search for the other two columns, under the command of General Nelson Cole and Colonel Samuel Walker, which were to meet them there.

Meanwhile, General Cole and Colonel Walker's columns had been marching north on the west and east sides of the Black Hills respectively. On the Belle Fourche River, to the north, they had met and joined forces. Then they had crossed to the Little Missouri River and continued west to the Powder. The meetings of the three columns had not gone as planned. Cole and Walker's men marched up and down the country looking for Connor's troops and missing them at every turn. In the meantime, they fought as many Indians as they could.

Although the three columns had originally been sent out to fight the Cheyenne, Connor had planned to use his soldiers to defeat all the Plains Indians in one fell swoop. He told his men that the Plains Indians were to be "hunted down like wolves," and gave them orders "to shoot and kill every male Indian over twelve years of age."

On August 14 Sitting Bull and the Hunkpapa met up with the joined forces of Cole and Walker for the first time.

Sitting Bull had gone out that day with a party of four hundred warriors. He knew the soldiers were nearby, and this time he was ready for them. But still he did not want to start a fight unless he was forced to. His scouts had told him that there were about two thousand soldiers, and he would have to act carefully.

When Sitting Bull sighted Cole and Walker's camp, he ordered some of his young men to approach the camp carrying a white truce flag. Then he waited to see what would happen.

Soon the young men came tearing back. The soldiers had fired at them; but the warriors had managed to escape, taking with them a few of the soldiers' horses.

These horses were sad-looking creatures—very thin and half-starved. As soon as he saw them, Sitting Bull knew that he and his warriors would be more than a match for the two thousand bluecoat soldiers. If their horses were in such bad shape, the men who rode them were probably not much better off.

Swiftly, silently, the Sioux warriors rode toward the soldiers' camp. They had learned much about fighting the white people since the battle on Where-They-Killed-the-Deer Mountain. This time they did not plan to face the soldiers directly. Instead they would surround them at a distance, dancing in on their swift horses to pick off a few bluecoats at a time with their arrows. Then they would retreat quickly, out of range of the soldiers' rifles.

The plan worked perfectly.

Cole and Walker's men were accustomed to fighting a solid line of soldiers. They were not accustomed to facing an enemy who appeared and disappeared in front of them like ghosts. The Indian ponies did their work well—weaving in and out of the soldiers' lines so quickly that they were but a whirl of dust. Before long the soldiers were ready to give up.

Cole and Connor's troops had been marching through the Powder River Valley for more than two months. As Sitting Bull guessed from the state of their horses, they were dangerously low on supplies. Hungry and fed up, they had lost the will to fight. Most of them had thought that fighting the Indians would be a great adventure. Now they only wished to escape with their lives.

When night fell, General Cole ordered a retreat all the way back to Fort Connor—a march of many days. He was afraid that if he did not, he would lose all his men. If Sioux arrows did not get them, then starvation surely would.

Sitting Bull and his warriors were filled with joy when they saw the soldiers leaving the next morning. For days they pursued the frightened bluecoats down the valley. But at last the soldiers met up with General Connor's troops near Fort Connor, where the expedition had begun, and the Hunkpapas decided to go home. They laughed at how the white soldiers had run away from them. The Hunkpapas had won an important victory. Next time the soldiers marched into their land, they were sure they could drive them out again.

General Patrick Connor, General Nelson Cole, and Colonel Samuel Walker would almost certainly have agreed. When they reached Fort Connor, which would later be renamed Fort Reno, they were, as one officer said, "as completely disgusted and discouraged an outfit of men as you ever saw." Their campaign had been a complete failure.

"The Indians," Connor telegraphed Washington, D.C., "have driven us out . . ." Before long, orders came back ordering Connor to disband the failed expedition. General Connor was sent back to his previous command at Salt Lake City, Utah. His blundering expedition had cost the United States government twenty million dollars—almost one million dollars for every Indian killed. And that was not even counting how many bluecoat soldiers had been lost. For the time being Sitting Bull and the other Sioux would be left alone.

But all was not calm.

The presence of the army had let loose a new restlessness across the plains. All the tribes were angry. And the angriest of all were the Oglala Sioux under their chief, Red Cloud. The Powder River Valley

Red Cloud, Oglala Sioux Chief

was their land—their last great hunting ground. They were furious that troops had been sent marching through it. Now they learned that because gold had been discovered in the Rocky Mountains of Montana, the white people planned to build a new road through their land. This road would allow miners to travel quickly and directly to the Rocky Mountains, and it would run straight through the Powder River country. Already the white people were building forts to guard this road, which they named the Bozeman Trail. Now regiments were marching out from Fort Laramie to build more forts farther west along the planned route of the new trail. In the spring of 1866 a peace commission was sent to meet with all the Indians living in the Powder River Valley to make a new treaty.

But Red Cloud did not want any part of it. Such a road would drive away the game that was left, and he had no intention of allowing it. "Great father sends us presents and wants new road," Red Cloud told the commissioners. "But white chief goes with soldiers to steal road whether Indian says yes or no."

This time Red Cloud made up his mind that he and his braves would fight every step of the way. They would make it as difficult as possible for the white people to enter their country, and even more difficult for them to stay there.

Red Cloud's war had begun.

9

The Battle for the Bozeman Trail

Sitting Bull and the Hunkpapas were too far north to take part in Red Cloud's war, but from Oglala visitors they heard how the fight for the Bozeman Trail had gone.

The white people had built two new forts along the trail. The first and larger one was called Fort Phil Kearny. The second one was Fort C.F. Smith. With these two forts the government believed it would have no trouble making the road safe for the miners and settlers who planned to use it. But Red Cloud and his warriors soon proved them wrong.

From lookouts along the hills, Red Cloud's braves watched the road with eagle eyes. They attacked any and all white people who tried to travel on it. These attacks were carried out so swiftly and so well that the soldiers could do little to stop them. By autumn, travel on the road had trickled down to almost nothing.

Now Red Cloud and his warriors turned their attention to the much-hated forts. They focused most of their energy on the larger and more important Fort Phil Kearny.

From hideaways in the hills and ravines, they watched the fort day and night until they knew as much about what went on there as the soldiers did. And they soon put this knowledge to use.

They did not try to attack the soldiers directly. Instead Red Cloud told his men to look for any sign of weakness, and then strike. Soon the men of Fort Phil Kearny discovered that anything foolish or reckless they did brought the wrath of Red Cloud's warriors upon them. A small group of men who went out alone, a horse left without a guard, or a careless sentry who poked his head over the fort walls were all easy targets for the watchful Sioux warriors. The commander of the fort, Colonel Henry B. Carrington, was soon forced to order his men not to leave the fort at all unless they absolutely had to, and even then, they were to be as careful as possible. But even this did little good. Red Cloud and his men were fighting for their nation and the future life of their people. And they were willing to do almost anything to win the fight.

As winter came the Sioux warriors hit upon a new tactic.

Now that the weather had turned cold, Colonel Carrington needed to keep up a supply of wood for the fort. For this reason, he regularly sent out parties of woodcutters to bring in wood from a nearby pine grove.

Knowing how important this wood was, Red Cloud's braves soon began attacking every wood "train" that came out. It was clear to Colonel Carrington that Red Cloud's braves would like nothing better than a fight with his soldiers. So he sent soldiers to guard the wood. The men had orders to maintain a tight guard around the wood trains no matter what. But some of the soldiers did not listen. And as one Oglala brave watched them, he got an idea of how the Indians might win a great victory against their enemy.

This brave noticed that some of the soldiers were careful and kept close together. But he also noticed that others behaved recklessly. These soldiers gave chase if they saw so much as a single Indian riding the ridges beside the trail. The brave decided that a few warriors could lead a group of these foolish soldiers over the hills to the place known as the

Lodge Trail Ridge. There it might be possible to ambush them. They could take the bluecoats by surprise and perhaps kill a great many of them.

The young brave's name was Crazy Horse. Sitting Bull and the Hunkpapas had been told about him by their Oglala relatives. He was the greatest warrior the Oglala Sioux had ever known.

Crazy Horse was a man of few words. Those who knew him said he had a strange air, almost as if he were not part of this world. He cared nothing for possessions and lived like a poor man, keeping only his horse and his bow and arrow. Sometimes Crazy Horse had visions where he dreamed himself into the world of spirits. To the Indians, the world of spirits was the true world, and everything on earth was but a pale shadow of it. At such times, his horse danced in a queer way so that it looked more like a whirling cloud of smoke than a flesh-and-blood animal. This is why he was given the name Crazy Horse.

Even though he was sometimes considered odd, he was the bravest of all Red Cloud's warriors. In battle, no one could touch Crazy Horse. For this reason, the Oglalas eagerly agreed to try his plan.

On December 21, 1866, Colonel Carrington sent out yet another group of woodcutters to fetch badly needed wood for the fort. As usual, Red Cloud's braves set upon this wood train. Carrington quickly organized a relief party of eighty-one soldiers. This party was under the command of a recent arrival at the fort, Captain William J. Fetterman. Colonel Carrington ordered Captain Fetterman to go to the aid of the wood train at once. Captain Fetterman was also ordered not to pursue the Indians beyond the Lodge Trail Ridge. His job was only to make sure the woodcutters, with their valuable loads of firewood, got back to the fort safely.

As Captain Fetterman and his men marched out from the fort to meet the line of supply wagons, Crazy Horse and a few other braves appeared on the ridge that ran above the trail. Shouting insults and waving red cloths in the air, they dared the soldiers to come and fight them.

At first the soldiers remembered Colonel Carrington's orders and did nothing. But at last Captain Fetterman found the temptation too much for him. He had been longing for the chance to fight some Indians. So, raising his rifle high, he shouted out boldly, "Come on, boys! Let's go get them!"

The young, handsome Captain William J. Fetterman was indeed one of those "foolish, reckless soldiers" Crazy Horse had noticed. The captain was known to think that no Indian could fight a white man and win. "Give me eighty men," he often boasted, "and I will ride through the whole Sioux nation!"

Now Captain Fetterman had his chance. For at his cry, all eighty-one men galloped after him over the hills in pursuit of Crazy Horse and the others. They were going toward Lodge Trail Ridge, which led over the hills north into the woods.

Captain Fetterman and his men raced over the wintry fields of tall grass, over the rocky ravines and ice-cold creeks, past whispering willow and cottonwood trees, toward the dark pine woods of the Lodge Trail Ridge. He and his men were fired up with excitement. They were sure that on this day they would at last manage to kill a few Indians. But no sooner had they crossed the ridge when they saw Indians leaping out at them from behind every rock, every tree, and every clump of grass. There were more Indians there than they had ever seen in their lives.

Later it was estimated that more than one thousand of Red Cloud's braves fought that day, and they made quick work of Captain Fetterman and his men.

Back at the fort, Colonel Carrington and the one hundred and twenty soldiers who had remained behind heard only a great volley of shots. Then an utter silence descended on the valley.

The next morning Carrington went out with his remaining men to fetch the bodies of Fetterman and his eighty-one soldiers. It was a bitterly cold day, and it looked like a blizzard was coming. In the freezing wind, the soldiers of Fort Phil Kearny loaded the bodies onto wagons and returned to the fort.

As night came, snow began to fall more and more heavily, piling up on the stockades and whirling icily through the air. Into the storm Colonel Carrington sent a courier, John "Portugee" Phillips. His orders were to ride to Fort Laramie and tell them of the massacre and plead for reinforcements. For four days Phillips rode through the blizzard. On the day after Christmas, he arrived at Fort Laramie, more dead than alive. And so it was that the outside world learned of the massacre of Captain William J. Fetterman and his eighty-one men. For the first time the

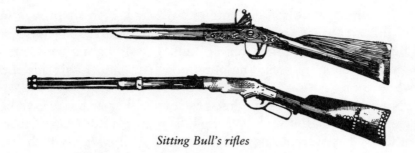

Sitting Bull's rifles

generals back East realized that Red Cloud and his braves meant business.

News of the battle, which the Indians named The Battle of the Hundred Slain, also spread quickly to the Plains Indians. Camps of Miniconjou, Sans Arc, and Brules Sioux all celebrated the great victory their people had won. But nowhere were the celebrations greater than in the Hunkpapa camp of Sitting Bull. The Oglala visitors who came with the news were made to tell the story of the battle over and over. In particular, Sitting Bull wanted to hear all about Crazy Horse, and he asked the visitors many questions about him. He felt as if he already knew this great warrior who, like him, often spoke to the Great Spirit Wakan Tanka. Together, Sitting Bull thought, he and this Crazy Horse might be able to keep the white people out of their land for all time. They might be able to save the unspoiled woods, mountains, lakes, and rivers, and all the animals that depended on them. Together they might be able to save their people's way of life. He longed to meet this Crazy Horse and to speak of these things with him.

But it was January, and the heavy snows of winter had come. Like the other Plains Indians, the Hunkpapas settled into their winter camp, cut off from everyone by the deep drifts of white that blanketed the world. For a long time they heard nothing of Red Cloud or his war. But in spring some surprising news came. A peace commission had come up the Missouri River to meet the Sioux camped there. This peace commission sent word that they wished to meet with Red Cloud at Fort Laramie in the middle of September. The white people wanted to make peace! For a time the Hunkpapas heard nothing new. Then, in late spring, some truly astonishing news came. Red Cloud had refused to meet with the peace commission! The white chiefs had been forced to pack up and go home again.

That summer Red Cloud's warriors resumed their fight for the Bozeman Trail. Now the Arapahos and the Cheyennes were fighting alongside them.

In August, with the help of these two other tribes, Red Cloud led attacks against both Fort C.F. Smith and Fort Phil Kearny. But these battles, which the white people named the Hayfield and Wagon Box fights, did not amount to anything. The soldiers could not drive back Red Cloud and his warriors. On the other hand, Red Cloud could not take these forts or persuade the soldiers to leave the safety of their high walls. The two sides were at a stalemate.

Nevertheless, the Bozeman Trail remained empty of travelers. And as long as this remained true, Red Cloud was winning the war; and the white people knew it.

In November 1867 the peace commissioners came back to Fort Laramie, but still Red Cloud refused to meet with them. This time, however, he sent them a message. He would talk of peace only when the white people had agreed to leave his country of the Powder River Valley forever and to close down the forts they had built there. Once again the peace commission was forced to go home without any agreement.

The white people were trying to make peace, but Red Cloud and his people were not making it easy for them. If peace was made this time, it would be on the Indians' terms.

10
The Treaty at Fort Laramie

For a long time Sitting Bull and the Hunkpapas heard nothing more of the white people's plan for peace. Red Cloud's war was still being fought. Then, one morning in May 1868, a Yankton scout named Blue Thunder arrived at the Hunkpapas' camp. He had a message from Fort Laramie.

The Hunkpapas liked to say that Blue Thunder's voice was so loud that whenever he spoke he had to cover his ears. Now he made an announcement in a voice loud enough for everyone in camp—and even beyond—to hear: A priest, or "black robe," was coming to tell them of the white people's new plan for peace. His name was Father Pierre Jean DeSmet. Would the Hunkpapas agree to welcome him?

For a long time no one said anything. At last Sitting Bull stepped forward. "Tell the Black Robe to fear nothing," he said. "We will welcome him and listen to what he has to say."

Father Pierre Jean DeSmet was due to arrive at the camp two days later. As was the custom, other bands of

Father DeSmet

Miniconjou, Sans Arc, and Brule Sioux came to join the Hunkpapas. Before long, more than three thousand Indians had gathered. The camp was buzzing with excitement, for everyone was eager to hear what the Black Robe would say.

Sitting Bull was chosen to be responsible for Father Pierre Jean DeSmet's safety. He was now considered a chief, and it was known that all the warriors would rather listen to him than to anyone else. When word came that the priest was drawing near, Sitting Bull mounted his favorite horse and rode out to meet him.

Father Pierre Jean DeSmet was a Jesuit missionary. A short, stocky, cheerful man, he had traveled among the Indians for many years. But even he was impressed by his first sight of Sitting Bull and his warriors. "Plumes of eagle and other birds adorned their long hair," he wrote, "mingled with silk ribbons and scalps captured from their enemies. Each one had his face daubed according to his own likes with black, red, yellow, and blue." The Hunkpapas were an impressive sight, but the most impressive of all was Sitting Bull.

Sitting Bull was more plainly dressed than the other Sioux. But his pride of bearing left Father Pierre Jean DeSmet no doubt that "he was generalissimo of the Sioux warriors." Although Sitting Bull now walked with a limp (the result of a bullet that had scraped the sole of his foot during a horse-stealing raid against the Crows two years before), every gesture he made gave an impression of enormous strength and force of will. Father DeSmet quickly decided that he must make his case to this man. The priest knew that if Sitting Bull agreed to meet with the commission, the others would follow.

For his part, Sitting Bull quietly took in the priest's broad smile and twinkling eyes. The Black Robe had an open, honest face, and the chief thought perhaps here was a white man who could be trusted. In the council meeting that night, he welcomed Father DeSmet with kind words.

"The whites provoked the war," he told the priest firmly, "with their injustices, their indignities to our families. The cruel massacre at Sand Creek shook all the veins which bind and support me. I rose up, tomahawk in hand, and did all the hurts I could. Today you are among us, and in your presence my arms stretch to the ground as if dead. I will listen to your good words, and . . . bad as I have been to the white men, just so good I am ready to become toward them."

Despite his warm welcome to the good priest, Sitting Bull was still wary. He listened carefully as Father DeSmet explained what the white people wished to do in this new treaty. Sitting Bull liked Father DeSmet, but he doubted that the other whites could be trusted. If the Hunkpapas sent a man to talk, he must be someone who would see straight, someone who would not be fooled by "soft words or sweet lies." For a long time, Sitting Bull thought about the problem. Then the answer came to him.

He would send his friend Gall, warrior chief of the Hunkpapas.

Even among the proud Sioux, Gall was an extraordinary figure. More than six feet tall, he had a chest like a wide barrel and thick arms that were as hard as newly forged iron. He had fought in many battles, and had received many an injury that would have killed a lesser man. Sitting Bull also remembered with satisfaction that Gall had no reason to love the white people.

Two years before, a group of white soldiers had come to arrest Gall on a charge of horse stealing. Gall had tried to escape out the back of his tepee, but the soldiers expected this and were there waiting for him. They attacked him with their bayonets, stabbing him many times through the body and once through the neck. Thinking he was dead, they kicked him again and again as he lay on the ground. Then they picked him up and tossed him into a nearby ravine.

It was January, and for many hours, Gall lay half-conscious and bleeding on the snow-covered ground. When he was sure the soldiers were gone, he somehow managed to pick himself up and walk about fifteen miles to the lodge of a famous medicine man.

When he arrived he was close to death. He was coughing up blood and still more blood streamed from his wounds. But the medicine man bound Gall's wounds with healing herbs, and by some miracle he survived.

Now Gall had recovered, but he had not forgiven or forgotten. For this reason, Sitting Bull thought he was sure to serve the Hunk-papas well.

Late that night, Sitting Bull called on Gall and arranged for him to go with Father Pierre Jean DeSmet back to Fort Laramie.

When Gall arrived at Fort Laramie, it was crowded with Indians and soldiers. All the chiefs, except Red Cloud, had come to hear the new treaty. Everyone waited restlessly to see what the great Red Cloud would do now.

Soon a message came. "We are on the mountains looking down on the soldiers and the forts," Red Cloud wrote. "When we see the soldiers moving away and the forts abandoned, then I will come down and talk."

The commissioners could not risk another failure. In August orders went out for the forts to be abandoned. A sad procession of soldiers

Chief Gall

formed along the Bozeman Trail, taking with them all their guns and possessions. Down from the hills came Red Cloud and his happy warriors. They fired flaming arrows at the forts, and watched silently until both forts had burned completely to the ground.

The war was won.

On November 6, 1868, Red Cloud and four hundred warriors rode in triumph into Fort Laramie. It was an unforgettable scene for the Indians who saw it. The sight of the lean, hawklike Red Cloud and his proud braves gave each of them a sweet sense of victory. From now on, the white people would not be so ready to steal Indian land.

The treaty, which was signed at Fort Laramie in November 1868, allowed the Sioux tribes to keep all the Dakota Territory west of the Missouri River and south of Parallel 46 as their own—a territory that covered all of present-day South Dakota west of the Missouri River. This land had at its heart the sacred country of Paha Sapa, the Black Hills. The land was to belong to the Sioux people for as long "as the grass shall grow and the waters shall flow." It was to form what the white people called the "Great Sioux Reservation." Within it, there would be agencies for all the different bands of Plains Indians, and the white people were to be forbidden from this land forever.

Red Cloud refused to sign the treaty until the Sioux also were given the rich Powder River country as their exclusive hunting grounds. This land lay north of the Platte River, east of the Bighorn Mountains, and stretched as far east as the western border of the Great Sioux Reservation. While this land was not given to them in a deed, it was to be under their control, and the white settlers were to be kept out of it. The Indians, who had never "ceded" this land to the United States government, considered it theirs and signed the treaty believing that was what the white people had agreed to.

In return for these things, Red Cloud also agreed to accept an additional reservation—to be named the Red Cloud Agency—in western Nebraska for himself and his people. Here the proud Oglala Sioux

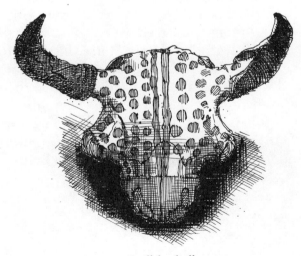

Buffalo skull

were to be overseen by an Indian agent from the government's Bureau of Indian Affairs. They would be "wild Indians" no longer. With this, Red Cloud and the other chiefs also pledged that "all war between the parties to this agreement shall forever cease."

Red Cloud's war was over.

After the treaty was signed, the Indian chiefs packed up and went home. Red Cloud prepared to move his people to their new home on the reservation. He had led his people wisely and well, but the victory he had won was bittersweet. Now he saw that the Sioux could not hope to keep their old way of life forever. The power of the white people was simply too great. If there was another war, Red Cloud had no doubt that the soldiers would win it. And so he advised his people to give up fighting and give in to the changes that had come. But for Red Cloud this was not a happy end to his long struggle. He told his people:

> *"You must begin anew and put away the wisdom of your fathers. You must lay up food, and forget the hungry. And when your house is built, your storeroom filled, then look around for a neighbor, whom you can take advantage of and seize all he has."*

With these words, one of the wisest and most farsighted of all the Sioux chiefs bitterly pledged himself to the white people's way of life. The time had come for peace.

But many of the warriors who had fought beside him did not agree. They had no desire to be penned up on a reservation with white agents to watch over them. Among these men were many of Red Cloud's finest warriors, including the legendary Crazy Horse. Instead of going to the Red Cloud Agency on the White River in Nebraska, these Indians moved north and west to the untamed lands promised them as hunting grounds, and into the hills of the Paha Sapa. There they joined forces with the other "wild Indians" who wanted nothing to do with the white people or their agencies. Of these, the most powerful were the Hunkpapas. And foremost among them was Sitting Bull.

11
Broken Promises

At the time of the Fort Laramie Treaty, Sitting Bull was willing to give peace a chance. But his heart soon turned hard again. A mere two years after the treaty had been signed, it was being broken. The "sweet words" the white people had whispered to the Indians at Fort Laramie meant nothing.

White settlers still clogged the trails west, and more of them came into Indian lands each year. The Americans were also building an "iron horse," as the Indians called the railroad—an extension of the Northern Pacific line, which at that time reached as far as the Missouri River at Bismarck, North Dakota. The tracks would run due west across presentday North Dakota. This territory was far north of the land promised the Sioux, but that was no comfort to Sitting Bull. This northern country was the home of the last great herd of buffalo. To the south the buffalo had already been killed off, cut down in the tens of thousands by the white people's bullets. If this great northern herd was destroyed as well, it would mean hard times for the Indians. Sitting Bull must have known that if the railroad came, it would not be long before the buffalo were gone.

A few years earlier, Sitting Bull had formed a new kind of warriors' club. The other Hunkpapas named this club The Silent Eaters. They met over meals, but none of the sounds of singing or laughter that usually went with Hunkpapa mealtimes ever came from their tepee. Instead one heard only the low, solemn murmur of men's voices. This was because the Silent Eaters met with a serious purpose in mind—to discuss the problems facing their people, and how to solve them.

The club met often these days, and the problem they discussed was always the same. How could they protect their land from the greedy white people who were coming at them from all sides?

"Iron horse"

It was useless to trust the treaty, Sitting Bull argued. The only hope for the Hunkpapas was to join with the other Indians of the plains and prepare to stand against the white people together.

The other Hunkpapas agreed, and soon their days were full of visits and meetings with other tribes—especially with the Oglala who had moved west with Crazy Horse.

Sitting Bull and Crazy Horse had become fast friends. Although Crazy Horse was a man of few words, the two understood each other well. Sitting Bull knew that, like him, the Oglala Sioux loved his country. He also knew that, above all, Crazy Horse wished to preserve the ancient ways of their people. Often the two spoke of what should be done. They both agreed that it would be wrong to start a war. But they believed that war would surely come eventually, and they must be ready. Someday the white people would try to break the treaty completely, and then they would send their soldiers.

It was only a matter of time. And that time came sooner than either of them expected.

In 1872 a general named D.S. Stanley was sent West to make a rough survey of the land and figure out a route for the next branch of the Northern Pacific railroad. After crossing from the Dakota Territory into Montana, he decided that the best route for the railroad to follow through the mountains was across the Yellowstone Valley. The tracks, he said, should be laid right along the south side of the river. But this territory was inside the unceded lands promised the Sioux as their exclusive hunting grounds for "as long as the buffalo shall roam there." That, however, did not worry Colonel Stanley or any of the others involved in planning the railroad.

In May 1873 a new peace commission arrived at Fort Laramie. They had come to ask the Indians' permission to build the branch of the railroad through the Yellowstone Valley.

The Sioux did not have to think about their answer for very long. "We want no railroad," they told the peace commission, "or any other white people's work on our land."

But the trouble did not stop there.

In June, when primroses and cactus flowers bloomed along the river banks, an army of fifteen hundred bluecoats came marching into the Yellowstone country. Their commander was once again General D.S.

General George Custer

Stanley. His orders were to lead a team of surveyors through the country and assure no harm came to them. The surveyors were to make a detailed map of Yellowstone to be used when work on the railroad started. It did not matter that the Indians had refused to give permission for the branch of the railroad to be built on their land.

Sitting Bull and Crazy Horse sent out scouts to follow the bluecoats. These Hunkpapa and Oglala braves hid behind rocks or in the tall grass. They watched the soldiers as they tramped over the land, scaring away the wild creatures with their marching feet and loud rifles. Once again their country was being invaded.

At the end of the summer Stanley completed his survey and returned East with his soldiers. He reported a "few skirmishes with hostile Indians." But no one was very worried about that. The survey was done. Now work on the railroad could begin.

But—perhaps fortunately for the white people—this work did not begin right away. The banks in the East were doing badly that year. A panic started, and rich people lost money. The plan for the railroad had to be put aside.

The white people, however, did not forget the Indian territory, and before long the soldiers were back.

In the summer of 1874 an army of one thousand came marching from Fort Lincoln, Nebraska. Their destination was the Black Hills— the sacred country that the Sioux had been promised would be theirs forever. The soldiers were part of the Seventh Regiment, the most experienced of the Indian-fighting troops. At their head was a man who was rapidly becoming the most famous Indian fighter of his day—General George A. Custer, or "Long Hair," as many Indians called him.

With his flowing golden locks and bright blue eyes, General Custer looked the part of a hero.

Only thirty-five years old, he had become a general during the Civil War, where he was known for his reckless courage. It was said of Custer that he did not know the meaning of the word *fear*. There were other Indian fighters who were almost as brave, and many who were far more effective. But Custer was the one who captured the imagination of the American people. In 1868 Custer had led his troops on a surprise attack against Black Kettle's Cheyennes (during which Black Kettle was killed) and defeated them. Ever since then, his every exploit had been eagerly followed by an adoring public. To them, Custer was all that a soldier should be—dashing, gallant, selfless, and brave. He was a nineteenth-century version of a storybook hero.

To the soldiers who worked under him, however, Custer was no hero at all. They found his fearlessness dangerous. Often he risked their lives for no good reason, and he seemed to care little for his soldiers' health or happiness. Worst of all, Custer frequently disbeyed orders, casting aside carefully laid plans in his quest for personal glory. General Stanley, who had commanded Custer on the march through Yellowstone, called him "a cold-blooded, untruthful, and unprincipled man." Many others felt the same. To be a hero, Custer did what he chose, and he never counted the cost for others.

Now this "hero" was marching into the sacred Black Hills. His orders were to explore the country and choose a good location for a new fort the U.S. Army wished to build there. It did not matter that these orders went directly against the Treaty of Fort Laramie. The government cared nothing for Indian rights. They wanted a fort to guard the men who would soon be coming to build the railroad, and a fort there would be.

Naturally the Sioux knew nothing of this, and they were puzzled to see the white soldiers come marching into their land. Puzzled and angry. Why had these soldiers come? What were they doing in *their* country?

Sitting Bull and Crazy Horse thought about the problem carefully. At last they decided to do nothing. They would watch and wait.

Once again, Indian scouts were sent out over the hills. They had orders to keep the bluecoats in their sight and report back everything they did.

For days the scouts kept General Custer and his men under close watch. But nothing these soldiers did made any sense. They did not look for Indians or try to fight the ones they saw. They only marched up and down the countryside like children playing a game. Sometimes they swam. Occasionally they fired their guns into the air. But most of the time, they just seemed to be looking around, disturbing the peace of Paha Sapa with their loud voices and careless ways.

One day a couple of the scouts saw the soldiers digging in the earth with strange tools of metal. The soldiers were acting very excited, as if they had discovered something wonderful.

The scouts found this very strange, and went back to tell the others. Most of the Hunkpapas could not imagine what it meant. But then, a few who were more familiar with the ways of the white people said the soldiers were probably looking for gold—the yellow metal that made the white people crazy. Most of the Hunkpapas began to laugh. Gold seemed to them a very foolish thing to get excited about. But they would not have laughed if they had known where this gold-seeking would lead.

On July 23 one of the men in Custer's company found a nugget of gold on the side of a high mountain that the Sioux had named Heen'ya Ha Ga, or Mountain Goat. The gold was a tiny amount, worth about ten cents. But that made no difference to General George Custer, who had a vivid imagination. By the time the expedition was over and he and his men were on their way back to Fort Abraham Lincoln, this small sliver of gold had been enlarged many times. There were reporters gathered around the fort to meet Custer and his men when they rode through the gates. Custer announced to them that the expedition had found "gold on every hillside, and from the grassroots down." There was, he said, enough gold in the Black Hills to make whoever went there a rich person.

Paha Sapa, land of peace and vision, was safe from the white people no longer.

As word of Custer's discovery spread eastward, miners and adventurers came racing toward the Black Hills from all directions, hungry for gold. By spring of 1875, more than a thousand of these men were camped in Paha Sapa, digging into its hills and riverbeds as fast as they could. Sitting Bull and Crazy Horse chased out as many of these intruders as possible. But more kept coming. Now both men were sure that the soldiers could not be far behind.

In September a Sioux half-breed named Louis Richards arrived at Sitting Bull's camp with a letter that he carried in the green pouch beside him. It was a message from the United States government. Richards read the letter out loud.

A new peace commission was coming to Fort Laramie. The government wished to purchase the Black Hills. The commission had come to find out how much money the Indians wanted for this land.

Sitting Bull did not wait to hear the rest of the letter. "I want you to go and tell the Great White Father that I do not wish to sell any land to the government," he said. Bending over, he picked up a pinch of dust in his fingers. "Not even," he added dramatically, "so much as this."

He refused even to meet with the commission.

At the Red Cloud Agency, the peace commissioners discovered that most of the Indians agreed with Sitting Bull. The mood was tense and unpleasant. Each day more angry young warriors gathered at the agency. In their hands were bows and arrows, ready to be fired. Many had rifles, too, and as they rode back and forth, they sang:

> *The Black Hills is my land*
> *And I love it*
> *Whoever interferes*
> *Will hear this gun*

They were not about to see their sacred land swallowed up by the greedy white people. The commissioners were frightened. They had not expected the Indians to have such strong feelings. They talked about the agreement they hoped to reach with the reservation chiefs. But even these peaceful Indians refused to sell. Then the commissioners offered simply to buy mineral rights to the land, which would allow them to go in and dig up the yellow metal they so prized. Still the answer was the same. The Black Hills country was the heart and soul of the Sioux nation. This land was not for sale at any price.

And so the commissioners were forced to pack up and go home. But their failure had made them angry. The commissioners told the United States Congress: If the Indians could not be persuaded to sell their land, the Congress should arrange to pay them "a fair equivalent for the value of the Black Hills." What they meant was: treaty or no treaty, and one way or another, the white people meant to have these hills with their wealth of gold.

Now, knowing the Sioux would not accept the "money" they meant to pay them, the government decided that it was time to make war and simply seize the land they so desired.

COURTESY NEW YORK PUBLIC LIBRARY

Major-General George Crook

In November E.C. Watkins, Special Inspector of Indian Affairs, reported that the Indians living in the unceded lands set out by the Fort Laramie Treaty were "well-armed and well-fed, lofty and independent in their attitudes." Calling these Indians "a threat to the peaceful reservation system," he said that troops should be sent out against them. The troops should "whip them into subjection," he wrote.

Shortly afterwards, Edward P. Smith, Commissioner of Indian Affairs, issued an order. It said that all Indians living freely in the territories that made up the Great Sioux Reservation and unceded hunting grounds, including the Black Hills, must report to their agencies (which were also in the Great Sioux Reservation) by January 31, 1876. If they failed to do so, troops would be sent out to force them in. This was a direct violation of the 1868 treaty. It meant that no Plains Indians would be allowed to live outside the control of U.S. government Indian agents any longer.

When the order came, Sitting Bull was camped at the mouth of the Powder River about two hundred and fifty miles from the western boundary of the Great Sioux Reservation. He knew at once what this order meant. It was a declaration of war. It was now December. Winter in the Powder River country was a harsh season of savage storms and brutal winds. Even if he wanted to, Sitting Bull knew it would be suicide to lead his people on such a journey at this time of year. The white people knew it, too. The messenger demanded that Sitting Bull reply to the order. The great chief said only that he would gladly bring his people in, but he could not do so until The Moon When the Green Grass Is Up, or early March, when the snows had melted. Sitting Bull looked calm as he watched the messenger ride off again, but inside his mind was racing.

War had come.

On February 7 the U.S. War Department declared that Sitting Bull, Crazy Horse, and the other Indians living in freedom in the Black Hills and other unceded lands had not come into their reservations. These Indians were "now to be considered hostile, and dealt with accordingly."

On March 17 General George "Three Stars" Crook came marching with a large army up the very Bozeman Trail that Red Cloud and his warriors had fought so bitterly to close ten years before. His target was Crazy Horse and his band of Oglala Sioux. However, on March 17 six companies of Crook's cavalry under Colonel J.J. Reynolds attacked instead a peaceful camp of Cheyennes led by Chief Two Moons. The Cheyennes did not have a chance. They fled up a steep hillside and watched as the soldiers set fire to their tepees, burning all they owned. They tried to fight back. But the soldiers had taken them by surprise and were too strong for them. At last those Cheyennes who had not been killed fled through the woods. Among them was Two Moons himself. He always had been opposed to war, but now he changed his mind. He led his people to the camp of Crazy Horse, about sixty miles away, up the Platte River.

When he reached the Oglala camp, Two Moons sought out Crazy Horse right away. "My people have been killed!" he told him, "My horses stolen. I am satisfied to fight." Crazy Horse's face showed no expression in the darkness. He only said that they must go and find Sitting Bull. The time had come for all of them to fight together.

12

Sitting Bull's Vision

In April Sitting Bull and the Hunkpapas were camped on the banks of the Powder River. Each day their camp grew larger as other bands came to join them for the fight against the white soldiers. Crazy Horse and the Oglalas arrived with the Cheyennes of Chief Two Moons. The Sans Arcs and the Miniconjous came. Many young men who had fled from reservations back East arrived. All had made up their minds to stop the white people from stealing the sacred land of Paha Sapa.

Day and night the camp hummed with activity. Scouts rode in with reports that the soldiers were marching toward them from all directions. Women busied themselves preparing enough dried meat and fruit to keep them from hunger in case they had to move quickly to stay out of reach of the soldiers. Serious-faced men counted up horses and weapons. And in Sitting Bull's Strong Heart lodge, warriors met late into the night and spoke of the days ahead.

Sitting Bull was the leader at these meetings. It was he who made everyone understand that the time had come to

Sioux Indian beadwork

join together and fight as one. "We are an island of Indians in a lake of whites," he told them. "We must stand together or they will rub us out separately." Oglalas, Miniconjous, Sans Arcs, and Brules listened and agreed with him. His strength and firmness gave them the confidence they needed to face the days ahead.

Yet sometimes, in private, Sitting Bull felt worried. Often alone, he rode out from the camp. At times like this he put the councils of war and the endless talk of warriors behind him. He rode high into the distant reaches of Paha Sapa where no human eyes were upon him. There he watched the eagle circle in the blue sky, or the lone wolf prowl among the rocks.

One day, alone on a high pass, he loosened the braids of his long hair. Taking out his long clay pipe, he filled it with tobacco and wound garlands of wild sage around its stem. Wild sage was a sacred herb to the Sioux. It was a symbol of all things mysterious and charged with the power of the Great Spirit. Slowly Sitting Bull lit the pipe. With the good smell of wild sage all around him, he smoked it. He tried to make his mind pure and empty so that Wakan Tanka, the Great Spirit, would be able to speak to him.

Silently he prayed. He prayed that his people might have plenty of food and that the land would be good to them. Most of all he prayed that Wakan Tanka would give him some sign of what he should do in the hard days of war ahead. He prayed that his people might be able to keep the country they loved. As he smoked the pipe, he sang his prayer:

Grandfather behold me!
Grandfather behold me!
I held my pipe and offered it to you
That my people may live

The annual Sun Dance, the greatest of all Sioux rituals, was to be held three days later on the banks of the Rosebud Creek. Sitting Bull was to take part in this Sun Dance, and he had promised to sacrifice a hundred pieces of his flesh to the Great Spirit. This was so that Wakan Tanka would take pity on Sitting Bull and give him the gift of vision. Now Sitting Bull prayed that this Sun Dance would be a good one.

The Sun Dance, as always, was to be held at the time when the June moon was full. This was the time, the Sioux believed, when the light of the Great Spirit was clearest—shining down brightly on the whole world.

For the Sun Dance a special lodge had to be built. This lodge was no ordinary building, but a copy of the entire universe.

It was in the shape of a circle, as the Sioux believed the universe to be. Twenty-eight poles held it up, and each of them stood for a different object in creation. One pole was the earth, another the heavens. There was a pole that stood for the sun, and another for the moon. There were also poles standing for each of the elements of our world—air, earth, fire, and water. Other poles symbolized animals that were important to the Sioux—the spotted eagle and the buffalo. The twenty-eight poles stood for the Sioux month as well, which followed the cycle of the moon.

In the center of the lodge stood a pole cut from the sacred cottonwood tree. This pole was a symbol of the tree that the Sioux believed stood at the center of the world. It led to Wakan Tanka, providing a bridge between heaven and earth. The sacred tree was a symbol for the center of all things, or the place where the Great Spirit dwelled. Medicine men taught that this center was not one place on earth. It was everywhere, within the souls of all men and women. When people understood this, the medicine men said, they would live in true peace. The cottonwood tree stood for this center because when it was cut one could see in its grain the perfect image of a five-pointed star— the Sioux symbol for the Great Spirit. It was also said that in even the lightest breeze, the branches of the cottonwood tree whispered and creaked in an endless song of prayer.

Once the sacred lodge was erected, the poles were hung with symbols made of rawhide. Then each pole was painted in a special way. Garlands of sage were twisted around them, and more sage was scattered on the floor. Only then was the lodge ready for the dancers.

When the lodge on Rosebud Creek was properly built, Sitting Bull and the other dancers were prepared for the ceremony of the Sun Dance. First they all smoked the sacred pipe of peace, sitting in a circle, as was the correct way. Then they were led to a sweat lodge. There water was poured over rocks that had been heated in the fire until they were red-hot. Steam rose up in clouds. The steam bathed the dancers and made them pure. When they were thought to be pure, they were led to the Sun Dance lodge. Their bodies were rubbed all over with wild sage, and each of them was painted with holy symbols. Sitting Bull's hands and feet were painted red, for red was the color of all things closest to the Great Spirit. Then blue stripes representing the sky were painted over his shoulders. Now he and the other dancers were ready.

Musicians began to play on whistles made of eagle bone. Soon the sacred drum started to beat. One at a time, the dancers were brought forward. Each of them was to be attached to the central pole by long rawhide thongs. The thongs ended in skewers, which were to be inserted under the skin of the chest. The dancers were to dance, pulling themselves away from the central pole, until they had broken free of these skewers. The Sioux believed the flesh stood for ignorance. Only by freeing themselves from the flesh in this harsh and painful manner could the dancers come close to the Great Spirit.

Before the Sun Dance began, however, each dancer had to sacrifice the pieces of flesh he had promised to the Great Spirit.

Sitting Bull stood still as a young warrior approached him with a sharp knife in his hand. The young warrior was none other than Kills-Often, the Assiniboine Sitting Bull had adopted as his little brother so

A Sioux flageolet, or flute

many years before. Working quickly, Kills-Often cut small patches of flesh from Sitting Bull's arms, chest, and back. Soon his entire body was covered with streaks of blood. Now the dance could begin.

Kills-Often led Sitting Bull into the sacred lodge. There young warriors strung four skewers through the muscles of Sitting Bull's chest. Then, grasping the rawhide thongs that streamed from them, they bound the thongs around the sacred pole at the center of the lodge. The shrill music of eagle-bone whistles filled the air. Along with the other dancers, Sitting Bull slowly began to bob up and down, fighting to free himself from the ties that bound him.

For three long days Sitting Bull danced. In the daytime he stared up into the blazing sun. At night he watched the cool round face of the moon. In all this time he was allowed nothing to eat. Blood flowed from his wounds, then grew sticky and hardened. The pain was terrible, but Sitting Bull did not once flinch or cry out. Instead he prayed. He called to Wakan Tanka to come to him, to speak to him.

At last, around noon, on the third day, Sitting Bull fell into a deep trance. He had broken himself free of the skewers that held him to the central pole. Weak and in pain, he stumbled to his knees. The world seemed to grow dark around him. Suddenly he heard a voice calling to him. "I give you these," the voice cried, "because they have no ears." Sitting Bull opened his eyes and looked up. To his amazement, he saw hundreds of bluecoat soldiers falling headfirst into the camp. They came down like grasshoppers from the sky, their hats falling off as they came.

When he awoke and the dance had ended, he told the others what he had seen. The other Hunkpapas knew immediately what Sitting Bull's vision meant.

Wakan Tanka was telling the Hunkpapas that he would give them these soldiers to be killed because the white people refused to listen when the Indians told them that the Black Hills were theirs to keep.

Sitting Bull and his people were about to win a great victory.

The Battle of the Little Bighorn

A fter the great Sun Dance, which was known forever after as the Sun Dance of Sitting Bull, the big camp of Indians moved to Ash Creek, which was between Rosebud Creek and the Little Bighorn River. From the pleasant camp among the willows and cottonwood trees, parties of young warriors were sent out each day to watch for the coming of the bluecoat soldiers.

One morning a group of warriors came racing back to camp. "Hiyu! Hiyu!" they cried. "The valley of the Rosebud is crawling with soldiers. Come!"

Sitting Bull and Crazy Horse quickly gathered their horses and set out.

Sitting Bull was still recovering from the Sun Dance, so that day Crazy Horse rode at the head of the warrior party. From his place farther back, Sitting Bull stared after his friend's horse, keeping it in his sight for as long as he could.

Long ago, when he was a boy, Crazy Horse had seen in a vision a great warrior whom neither arrows nor bullets could touch. On this day, he was dressed like the warrior of his vision. White hailstones were painted all over his body. Across his face ran a red thunderbolt. In his hair was a bonnet made of the feathers of the red-backed hawk. And behind his ear was tied a small brown pebble, a magic charm that he believed would keep him from harm.

As Sitting Bull watched, Crazy Horse seemed to will himself into the world of spirits, becoming the warrior of his vision. Spurring the others forward, he taught them that day how to fight against the white soldiers as they never had before. With Crazy Horse leading them, Sioux and Cheyenne braves swept into the valley of the Rosebud, swooping down on the lines of bluecoat soldiers like fierce eagles. They struck so quickly, and from so many directions, that the battle had not gone on long before the soldiers became confused and frightened. Slowly they began to retreat up into the woods. At last darkness fell. Then their commander, the fierce-eyed General George Crook, ordered them to back off entirely. Crook was perhaps the toughest and most experienced Indian fighter in the country. But even he had no chance against Crazy Horse that day.

The Sioux and Cheyenne had won a major victory.

That night the camp at Ash Creek was full of rejoicing as young men and old gathered to congratulate Crazy Horse. Sitting tall and straight on his black horse, Crazy Horse gravely accepted their praise.

During the night many sought out Sitting Bull and asked him: "Is this the victory you dreamed of?" But Sitting Bull said no. That victory was yet to come.

In the Sioux calendar, June is the Moon When the Chokeberries Are Ripe. With the soldiers gone, the Indians moved to their favorite summer camp. It was a place they called Greasy Grass, on the wide green banks of Little Bighorn River.

By now the camp had grown to an enormous size. Some bands of Western Sioux were there, along with the Cheyennes and the Arapahos. Altogether there were about twelve thousand Indians—so many that when they set up camp along the river, their circles of tepees stretched for a distance of more than three miles.

For several days the Indians rested. Women played with children by the river. Boys swam and men fished. But even so, there was tension in the air. Everyone was wondering when the next fight with the soldiers would come.

The morning of June 25 dawned quiet and sunny. Everyone was working. Suddenly a cry went up: "The Chargers are coming! The Chargers are coming!" Quick as wildfire, the news spread from band to band. The bluecoats were marching over the hills on the other side of the river, coming straight toward the camp!

The approaching soldiers were none other than the Seventh Regiment. The regiment was led, once again, by General George A. Custer.

Custer had changed little since his march through the Black Hills two years before. He was still hungry for glory. But now he had even more pressing reasons for wanting to prove himself. Custer was in disgrace. He had offended a very important man—the president of the United States, Ulysses S. Grant.

At that time, there was talk of scandal in President Grant's government. It was said that bribery and stealing of public money existed all through his offices, even among those who were in charge of the Western territories. Many claimed that even the president's own brother was involved. Custer, who could never resist being the center of attention, said that he had secret information that proved it. He was called before the Congress to testify. But there it soon became clear that Custer's "secret information" was nothing more than gossip. He knew nothing of any importance at all. When President Grant realized this he was furious. He sent orders that Custer should not be allowed to lead the Seventh Regiment when they next went out against the Indians.

Instead he was to remain at Fort Lincoln, Nebraska, until Grant decided what to do with him. It looked as if Custer's glorious career was over. But then Custer begged General Alfred H. Terry, the man President Grant had chosen to lead this latest war against the Indians, to help him.

General Terry was a kindly man who looked more like an absent-minded professor than a hardened soldier. He felt sorry for Custer and agreed to help him. Terry asked President Grant to give the hot-headed young general one more chance. Custer might be a foolish man in

COURTESY MUSEUM OF THE AMERICAN INDIAN, HEYE FOUNDATION

General George Custer

private life, Terry said, but he *was* a brave soldier. At last President Grant gave in. If Terry wanted him, Custer could go with his old Seventh Regiment, under Terry's command, to fight the Sioux.

Unfortunately, this experience did not make Custer any more humble or any better at obeying orders. While Custer must have felt grateful to General Terry, it was not long before he was disobeying him at every turn.

General Terry was convinced that the Indians were camped on the Little Bighorn River and hoped to trap them there. For this reason, he ordered Custer to march his men up Rosebud Creek to its head. Once there he was to cross over west to Little Bighorn River and march down it from the south. Meanwhile, another force, commanded by Colonel John Gibbon, would be marching south along the Bighorn River to its junction with the Little Bighorn River. If both men timed their marches correctly, Custer's forces should then be able to drive the Sioux warriors north, where Gibbon's forces would be waiting for them.

It was a sound strategy, but Custer was not about to follow it.

Instead of leading his men all the way up to the head of the Rosebud, on June 24 Custer ordered them to turn west toward the Little Bighorn. He had made up his mind to take on the forces of Sitting Bull and Crazy Horse on his own. He was not going to wait for Gibbon's forces to get in position. Instead, he planned to get there ahead of them. This victory would belong to his Seventh Regiment alone. Once Custer had defeated the rebel chiefs, everyone would know that he was indeed the greatest Indian fighter of the West. After that, even President Grant's anger would not mean much.

And so Custer ordered his men to march toward the Little Bighorn River as fast as they could.

The men of the Seventh Regiment rode quickly over the dusty hills and ravines that led to the divide between the Rosebud and the Little Bighorn. Along the way many of Custer's men spoke with excitement of the battle that was to come. This time they would show the Indians what real fighting men could do! But others were not so sure. They noticed that the Indian scouts leading them were starting to behave strangely. At one point these scouts told the soldiers that they would show them where the valley was, but they would not lead them into it. When some of the soldiers asked why, the scouts took them to a place where a picture had been drawn in the sand. The picture showed soldiers falling from the sky into an Indian camp full of tepees. This picture, the scouts said, told that the Indians would win a great victory—perhaps at the Little Bighorn. When they heard this, a few of the soldiers became frightened. They tried to tell General Custer what the scouts had said. But Custer paid no attention.

On the morning of June 25, Custer and his men reached the divide between Rosebud Creek and the Little Bighorn Valley. There, Custer decided to divide his force of about six hundred and thirty men. He ordered Captain Frederick Benteen, one of his best officers, to lead three companies of one hundred and twelve men south to scout for Indians. "Look for them everywhere," he ordered Benteen, "and attack any you find."

When Benteen and his men had gone, Custer and the other leading officer of the regiment, Major Marcus A. Reno, continued toward the Little Bighorn with the remaining troops. Over the hills they marched as the sun climbed in the sky. Suddenly Custer caught sight of a huge cloud of dust rising over the plain from the other side of the Little Bighorn River. It never occurred to Custer that this dust might be from a large Indian camp containing many fires and horses moving about. Instead he cried excitedly to Major Reno, "There are your Indians! Running like the devil!" He then ordered Reno to take three more troops of one hundred and twelve soldiers and give chase immediately. "We will come up behind to support you," Custer cried after Reno jauntily. It was the last time Reno ever saw Custer alive.

The Indians first realized that the bluecoats really *were* going to attack when Reno's men galloped over the hill. The cavalry charged down to the riverbed and began firing their guns up at the south end of the Indian camp, which lay north of them.

The south end was where the Hunkpapas were, and the first shots took them completely by surprise. "I did not believe it," one man said later. "I did not think it possible that any white man would attack us strong as we were . . ." But within moments, bullets were whizzing everywhere, and quickly the Hunkpapa warriors sprang into action.

At their head was the fierce Gall. Reno's first volley of bullets had killed his wife and three of his children. "It made my heart bad," he told reporters years later. Armed with nothing but his hatchet, he raced out like an angel of death to meet Reno and his men.

The other warriors followed close behind. With their bows, arrows, axes, and tomahawks, they sliced through Reno's forces like a knife through butter. Reno ordered his men to get off their horses and try to hold the Indians back. But it did no good. The Sioux warriors were soon all over them. Reno's men were forced to get on their horses again and retreat across the river and into the bluffs. Almost half of Reno's men had been cut down.

Meanwhile, to the north where the Cheyenne were camped, women and children watched in amazement as Custer and his men rode down a coulee to the river. They could not believe these white soldiers were preparing to charge right into the center of their camp, where already warriors were massing to strike.

Sioux and Cheyenne braves quickly mounted their horses and galloped across the river to meet Custer and his men. When Custer and his troops saw how many Indians were coming, they started to withdraw up the ridge to higher ground. But it was too late. From the south came the Hunkpapas. They were led by Gall, who, seeing more soldiers, had raced furiously north to meet this new attack. From the north and east came Crazy Horse and the Oglalas, their horses pounding toward the soldiers as fast as lightning.

Together these warriors swarmed over Custer and his men, in the words of one Blackfoot chief, "like a hurricane . . . like bees swarming out of a hive." Custer and his men retreated up the slopes to a hilltop east of the river. But soon the Indians caught up with them. "They tried to hold on to their horses," said a Hunkpapa warrior named Crow King, "but as we pressed them closer they let go (of) their horses." After that all was chaos. The air filled with dust and gunpowder. Horses stampeded wildly this way and that. Arrows fell thick as rain and screams and cries could be heard on all sides. There was so much smoke that it was several minutes before the Indians realized they were firing at nothing.

Custer and all his men were dead.

Said Crow King later of Custer and his soldiers: "We crowded them toward our main camp and killed them all. They kept in order and fought like brave warriors as long as they had a man left."

Sitting Bull's prophecy had come true.

To the south, Reno and his men were still struggling for their lives. Gall's first attack had driven them back across the river and to the top of the bluff. Many men had been lost, and those still alive were frightened and disorganized. All might have been lost had not Captain Frederick Benteen ridden up at that moment. He had failed to find any Indians on his scouting trip south, and was looking to rejoin the rest of the troops.

"For God's sake, Benteen, help me!" Reno cried, "I've lost half my men."

Benteen immediately got off his horse and took charge. He was an excellent officer, known for his nerves of steel. Quickly he set about organizing a defense. He ordered his and Reno's men to dig themselves in on the top of the bluff and along the hillsides to wait for the next Indian attack.

This attack was not long in coming, and when it came it was a furious one. Sioux warriors and soldiers fought on the bluff and hillsides. With each hour more soldiers fell dead and wounded. But when darkness came and the Indians pulled back, Reno and Benteen's men still held their position along the bluff leading down to the river. The fight would continue the next morning.

Sitting Bull and Gall were sure they would win. They surrounded the hill where Reno and Benteen's men were camped, and settled down to wait for sunrise when they would attack again.

In the camp, great fires were being lit as the Indians celebrated their victory over Custer and his men. Drums beat out the story of the battle in a fast and furious rhythm. Warriors young and old danced and made up kill-songs telling about General Custer. The thief who had marched so boldly into the sacred Black Hills had been defeated at last. "Long Hair is dead," they sang, "Where he lies, nobody knows."

But all were not celebrating.

Sitting Bull stood watch over the hillside where lights from the camp of Reno and Benteen could be seen faintly in the darkness. From his post he ordered scouts to go running through the night, searching the hills all around to see if any more soldiers were coming. Meanwhile, he and his warriors stayed alert, watching the sky for the first trace of light that would signal morning.

Dawn comes early during the plains summer. It was only 2:35 in the morning when the first rays of sunlight began to appear to the east, casting a pale, spidery light over the now silent valley.

It was time to go back to the fight.

Silently Sitting Bull, Gall, and the other warriors mounted their horses and sped up the hillside. They attacked with great energy. During the night, however, the soldiers had dug themselves like moles deep into the bluff and the hillsides, and it was hard to draw them out. Still, as the sun rose in the sky, it became clear that the Sioux were winning. With each passing hour, they drew closer and closer to the soldiers. It was only a matter of time before they would swarm over them, driving them out of their hiding places.

But suddenly, around noon, a young Sioux boy came riding over from the camp. The scouts had returned, he said. They reported many soldiers approaching from the north. Sitting Bull turned to the others and told them that it was time to return to camp. The Indians were not ready for another fight with the soldiers. They must prepare to move now—before the bluecoats reached them.

And so the warriors turned their horses and rode away, letting Reno and Benteen's troops escape with their lives.

Across the river, women worked quickly to pull down tepees and pack up belongings. Men raced to gather together horses and weapons. At last all was ready. To cover their trail, the Indians set fire to the tall prairie grass along the riverbank. A huge cloud of smoke rose up over the plain. Behind this wall of smoke, Sitting Bull and the others made their escape from Little Bighorn valley.

Moving with great speed and grace, the bands of Sioux and Cheyenne disappeared one by one into the high rolling plains to the southwest of the Little Bighorn. Peering through the smoke, the survivors of the Seventh Regiment watched them go.

The greatest battle of the West was over.

The Indians of the plains had beaten their enemy badly. But as they made their way toward the Big Horn Mountains, their mood was far from happy. Although some of the young warriors continued to sing their kill-songs and boast of the coups they had taken, the rest fell into an uneasy silence. Sitting Bull was among them. He had won the victory he had been promised by the Great Spirit, but what would happen now? There were many white people, more than all the Indians put together. What would they do when they learned how badly they had been beaten at the Little Bighorn?

14

A New Home

On the night of June 26, Lieutenant James Bradley, who was in charge of Indian scouts on the expedition, told General Terry that some of his Crow scouts said there had been a great battle farther down the Little Bighorn. According to these scouts, "all the pony soldiers had been killed." General Terry and John Gibbon did not believe the scouts' story. But as there was no word of Custer, it did seem likely that there had been heavy fighting.

At daybreak the next morning Terry and Gibbon led their troops marching toward the place where the scouts said the battle had taken place. Lieutenant Bradley was sent ahead with the Crow scouts. Reno and Benteen sighted the approaching forces of Terry and Gibbon from miles away. They were afraid it might be the Indians returning, so they sent a pair of officers across the river to find out who was coming. When these officers saw General Terry, they cried out: "Where is Custer?"

Neither Terry nor Gibbon could give them an answer. No sooner had they reached Reno and Benteen when Lieutenant Bradley rode up with a couple of Indian scouts.

Bradley told them that he had been up in the hills on the east bank of the Little Bighorn when he had spotted a huddle of shapes. He had thought they were buffalo carcasses, left over from an old hunt. But when he drew closer, he realized that they were not buffalo skeletons, but the bodies of men and horses—all dead.

Custer and his men were no longer missing.

Terry and Gibbon sent messengers racing to forts all along the frontier with news of the massacre. From these forts, word of Custer's death traveled rapidly East by telegraph. Before long the entire nation learned how brave General Custer and two hundred and thirty-five men of the valiant Seventh Regiment had met their deaths at the hands of a bunch of "savage Indians" in a distant valley in Montana. These Americans, knowing nothing of why the Indians were fighting, cried out as if in a single voice for revenge. Revenge for Custer's murder and death to the Indians!

The once empty trails and quiet hills of the Sioux country were now filled with the echo of marching feet as the bluecoats moved like a well-oiled machine to crush the "savages" who had so shamed them.

It was not long before Sitting Bull and his people had to run endlessly from place to place dodging the soldiers and their rifles. Crazy Horse and the Oglalas ran with them until the two bands decided it would be safer to split up. Crazy Horse went with the Oglalas to Bear Butte, on the plains northeast of the Black Hills. Bear Butte was known to be a sacred place and Crazy Horse believed the Great Spirit would protect his people there. Sitting Bull and the Hunkpapas, meanwhile, traveled northwest to the lower Yellowstone country. But no matter how far they went, it seemed as if there was nowhere to hide. Now, Sitting Bull and Crazy Horse learned what Little Crow and Red Cloud had learned years before:

> *"See, the white men are like locusts when they fly*
> *so thick that the whole sky is a snowstorm. You*
> *may kill one—two—ten; yes, as many as the*
> *leaves in the forest yonder, and their brothers*
> *will not miss them. Kill one, two, ten—and ten*
> *times ten will come kill you."*

There were too many white people, and the Indians could not hope to fight them all.

Sitting Bull had always been a brave man, ready to face whatever came. But now his heart felt as heavy as a stone in his chest. The Great Spirit had given him a vision, a great vision that had come true. But now, no matter how hard he prayed, he could see nothing. Only war and death.

In September Sitting Bull and the Hunkpapas heard from their Oglala friends how General "Three Stars" Crook had led an attack on the camp of the Oglala chief, American Horse, at Slim Buttes to the north of the Black Hills.

Crazy Horse and his warriors had set out as fast as they could to help American Horse and his people. They planned to give the soldiers a good fight.

But when they reached the camp, hope died.

The soldiers were there all right—a line of them stretching as far as the eye could see. "Like a forest of pine trees," the Oglalas said later. Although Crazy Horse and his braves fought hard, they could not break through the line of bluecoats. This time, "Three Stars" Crook had more than enough men to stand against the Sioux braves. The fighting continued until American Horse, mortally wounded, was forced to surrender. Then, as the Indians watched, the soldiers set fire to American Horse's camp, and continued on to the Black Hills.

Galloping as fast as they could, the Oglala warriors rode toward the camp where flames leaped and crackled all around. Crazy Horse and his warriors got off their horses and slowly walked around the burning camp. Crazy Horse found an old woman wrapped in a blanket. "Are you living?" he cried, shaking her. She fell over at his touch, shot through the head. A young girl was beside the old woman. She, too, was dead, as was a baby in her arms. In a bale of hay, they found the body of an eleven-year-old boy, also dead. Among the bodies were many faces they recognized—Red Water Woman, Swift Bear, Little Eagle. The names seemed to wail out at them from the wind and the flames.

When Sitting Bull heard of the massacre he was filled with anger and grief. "What is it the white people want of us?" he cried in despair, looking around at his family and friends. "We have been running up and down this country, but they follow us from one place to another."

No one said anything in reply.

Through the autumn, Sitting Bull and his people continued to run and hide like creatures of the wild. In October news came from the East. The Great White Chief in Washington, D.C., had forced the chiefs on the reservations to sign a treaty giving up not only the Black Hills, but also the Powder River Valley. Sitting Bull and the other "wild" Indians had nowhere to go but the reservations. And this Sitting Bull hoped never to do.

When Sitting Bull heard the news he called all his people together. Young and old came and gathered, waiting to hear what he would tell them. Small children sat and listened with serious faces. Mothers with babies in their arms looked at him with wide eyes. Warriors sat silent. "My people," Sitting Bull began, "we can go nowhere without seeing the head of an American. Our land is small, it is like an island in a lake. We have two ways to go now. South to the land of the Spaniards, or north to the Land of the Grandmother."

When they heard this, everyone began talking at once. The land of the Spaniards was far, far away—so far that none of the Hunkpapas had ever been there. But the Land of the Grandmother, as the Sioux called Canada because it was ruled by Queen Victoria, was not so far. Some of the Hunkpapas had even visited there. Perhaps in that country they might find a peaceful home. Across the Medicine Road, as the Sioux called the Canadian border, were the wide, empty plains of Saskatchewan. There were cool pine forests there and rushing rivers of clear water. It was a wild and beautiful land. Perhaps there they could be happy again.

As the leaves changed color and the air grew chilly, Sitting Bull and his people moved northward, hunting buffalo and dodging the white soldiers. Late in October a young, ambitious colonel named Nelson Miles caught up with the Hunkpapas on the high bluffs of the Yellowstone Valley and asked for a meeting.

On a cold, windy day Sitting Bull and the colonel met with soldiers on one side and Hunkpapa warriors on the other. Colonel Nelson Miles told Sitting Bull that there would be no peace for his people until he surrendered and came with them to a reservation. Sitting Bull looked the colonel up and down. "God made me an Indian," he replied with pride. "But he did not make me an agency Indian, and I do not intend to become one."

When Miles realized that Sitting Bull would not come to the reservation with him, he ordered his soldiers to open fire. Once again the Hunkpapas had to run for cover, racing up and down the hills to stay away from the soldiers' guns. But now they had made a decision. They could live in the land they had been born in no longer. It was time to go to a new home.

Before leaving, the Hunkpapas tried to find Crazy Horse and his band of Oglalas to ask them to join them on their journey to Canada. But Crazy Horse and his people had moved south. And even though they searched for them for a long time, the Hunkpapas could not find them anywhere. At last they gave up and prepared to make the journey to a new land.

Before he left, Sitting Bull made sure to say goodbye to the country of his fathers. He rode out alone far and wide, to places he had known as a boy and as a young man. He passed by favorite streams and trees he was particularly fond of, and to each he said his farewells. One day, when he was out riding around, he saw a lonely gray wolf climbing over the rocks. The wolf was muttering to itself, and when he listened closely Sitting Bull heard that it was singing a song:

> *I am a lonely wolf*
> *Wandering pretty nearly all over the world*
> *What is the matter, you say?*
> *I am having a hard time, friend*
> *All alone wandering*
> *And so will you*

Sitting Bull sang the wolf's song to himself until he knew it by heart. That was what he was now—a lonely wolf with no home of his own.

Shortly afterwards, he and his people crossed the Medicine Road and into the Land of the Grandmother.

In the beginning their new home was peaceful. There was no need to fight there, and for the first time in many years Sitting Bull and the other warriors could settle back and enjoy their families.

Sitting Bull had two wives now, many children, and even grand-children. The newest addition to his family was a set of twins—newborn baby boys. They grew fast, and Sitting Bull never became tired of playing with them. He liked to tease them by telling them the old Sioux tales of

Sitting Bull and wife

owls who liked to kidnap little Indian children and eat them for supper. When he was not busy with his own family, he spent much time with the young men of the tribe. He tried to tell them how to be brave, strong-hearted, and good. He told them old legends and tales of the world before the white people came. He wanted to keep alive in these young men the old ways of his people, which he believed were in danger of being lost in this new land.

The Hunkpapas made a happy beginning in the Land of the Grandmother. But as time passed, troubles began.

Many of the Hunkpapas grew homesick. Try as they might, they could not forget the land where they had been born. Although the Land of the Grandmother was beautiful, it did not have the same skies or fields or mountains as their old country. There, too, the spirits did not speak as they had in their own land. Also, the buffalo, which had always supported them, no longer roamed that far north in any great numbers. The Hunkpapas tried to catch what other game they could—deer, elk, and even jackrabbits—but they often went hungry. And even when there was food, no one could forget the taste of fresh buffalo meat—a taste they all hungered for and missed as a way of life now gone.

Worse still the land they now lived on did not belong to them. They were guests of the Canadian government. The Canadians told them that they would only be welcome so long as they behaved themselves and were able to catch enough wild game to feed themselves. Over and over again, Sitting Bull went to speak to the Canadians to ask them to give his people just a small piece of land they could call their own. But the answer was always the same. "You can expect nothing at all from the Queen's government," the Canadians told him. "Your only hope is the buffalo and it will not be long before that source of supply ceases."

Then, in late 1877, Sitting Bull had something new to worry about. The American government was embarrassed that Sitting Bull and his people had been forced to live in exile. The Americans wanted them to come back home, and asked the Canadians to help them persuade the Hunkpapas to do so.

In September a commission led by General Alfred H. Terry arrived at Fort Walsh on the Canadian-American border. He had been sent to tell Sitting Bull that the time had come for him and his people to surrender. His orders were to persuade them to come back to America and live on a reservation.

At first Sitting Bull refused to meet with this commission. He had no reason to trust the Americans, he told the Canadian police. They had always lied to him before. And there was no doubt in his mind that they would lie to him again this time. But the Canadian Mounted Police did all they could to persuade the chief to meet with the Americans. It could not hurt to talk, they argued.

Because Sitting Bull felt that the government of Canada had treated him kindly, he agreed.

In late October he and a large group of his people arrived at Fort Walsh.

General Terry opened the meeting by saying that this war between the Indians and the Americans had gone on long enough. It was time for Sitting Bull—the last holdout—to make peace.

Chief Sitting Bull

Sitting Bull's reply rang through the room. "The part of the country you gave me," he told Terry and the others, "you ran me out of. I have now come here to stay with these people and I intend to stay . . ."

General Terry and the other commissioners could not honestly deny Sitting Bull's charge. But they still did their best to persuade him to return. They reminded him that he and his people owned nothing in Canada. They reminded him that America was his home. But Sitting Bull would have none of it. He called on members of his tribe to stand and speak.

In simple, rich language the Hunkpapas spoke of what the Americans had done to them. They told of how their lands had been stolen and their people killed. Even the buffalo, which had always given them food and clothing, had all been shot down by the white hunters. The last to speak was a woman. Women were almost never allowed to speak in Indian councils. This time, however, Sitting Bull made an exception. The woman, who ever after was called She-Who-Speaks-Once, rose gracefully and began in a low, musical voice: "I was over in your country," she said. "I wanted to raise my children there, but you did not give me any time. I have come to this country to raise my children, and have a little peace."

After that the commissioners knew that no matter what arguments they used, they could not persuade Sitting Bull and his followers to surrender. And so the commissioners packed up and went home.

But for the Americans the visit had not been a total loss. They had asked the Canadians to promise that they would never give Sitting Bull and his people a permanent home in their land. The Canadians did not want trouble with their powerful American neighbors, so they agreed. The Hunkpapas were still a people without a land of their own. Because of this, times soon became hard.

The winter of 1881 was the coldest anyone could remember. Ice and snow covered the world. The air became blue and still. It was so cold that many of the Hunkpapa ponies got sick and died. Without horses it was impossible to hunt enough game, and soon the whole camp was hungry.

At first they survived by buying supplies from traders on credit. But after a while the traders would not give them any more goods until they brought in new fur pelts or buffalo hides. The Hunkpapas traded everything they had—finely worked buffalo robes, belts of beads and feathers, even sacred ornaments. It was not long before they had nothing left to give. Now they began to starve.

A few families packed up and went south across the border. There they surrendered to the Americans and were taken to a reservation. As the winter passed, more families joined them. Spring came, but all was still cold and barren. Now the Hunkpapa began returning to America in great numbers, among them some of Sitting Bull's closest friends and followers. When the first shoots of grass appeared on the prairie, Gall, the great war chief, set off on the long march south. He had always been

Sitting Bull's right-hand man and his most trusted lieutenant. But even he told Sitting Bull that he could not stay. Life in America might not be good, he said, but at least there was food to eat.

Sadly, Sitting Bull watched his friend go. He understood why so many of the Hunkpapas were leaving. But he could not bear the idea of surrendering. He had always promised never to become an agency Indian—an Indian who looked up to white people as his masters. But what was he to do? Of the three thousand who had crossed with him into Canada, only one hundred and eighty-seven remained. These people were all half-naked, cold, and hungry. What was left for them?

At that time the main trader in the Saskatchewan district was a French Canadian named Jean LeGare. A shrewd man with dancing black eyes and sharp features, LeGare was known for his honesty. Despite his general mistrust of white people, Sitting Bull liked and trusted him. Therefore, he went to visit Mr. LeGare to ask his advice.

LeGare's reply was direct and to the point. "My friend," he told Sitting Bull, "you are poor and you will not be able to live much longer here. Take my word for it, your only hope is to surrender."

Sitting Bull said nothing for a long time. He was thinking back, remembering all that he had seen and done. He thought of his father and of the old days fighting the Crows. He thought of the Sun Dance on the Rosebud River and of the great victory he and Crazy Horse had won at the Little Bighorn. At last, he said: "Very well, I will go with you. I trust you, but not the Americans. If you take me south to their country, I will go."

On July 10, 1881, Sitting Bull and his one hundred and eighty-seven followers set out on the journey south. Jean LeGare accompanied them, driving an old wooden wagon. The journey took nine days. By the time they crossed the border and arrived at Fort Buford, where the surrender was to take place, Sitting Bull and his remaining followers were half-dead from hunger and exhaustion. To the reporters who had gathered to see the famous Sitting Bull, the man they met was something of a disappointment. He did not look like the fierce, proud warrior chief of their stories and legends. Instead he had the face of a tired, old man. He was dressed simply in a torn calico shirt and a pair of dirty leggings. He stood apart from the others, waiting until everyone else had handed over their weapons. Then, at last, he gave his old rusty Winchester rifle to his small son, Crow Foot, and told him to go and give it to the white soldiers. After that he allowed himself to be led away quietly.

He was the last member of his tribe to surrender to the government of the United States of America. Now he must become what he had always hated—an agency Indian.

15
The Last Indian

When Sitting Bull surrendered, the blue-coats promised him that he would go to live with his people at the Sioux reservation in Standing Rock, North Dakota. But when he handed over his rifle, they put handcuffs on him. He became a prisoner of war, charged with the murder of General George A. Custer. His new home would be the stockades of Fort Randall, more than three hundred miles away, on the banks of the Missouri River.

The soldiers escorted Sitting Bull and his two wives to a steamboat that would take them down the river to the fort. It was a long, sad journey. Sitting Bull was sure the white people planned to kill him as soon as he reached Fort Randall. He had heard how his friend Crazy Horse had been murdered several years before at Fort Robinson. The fearless Crazy Horse had not died in battle but as a prisoner—stabbed to death by the soldiers. Sitting Bull was sure that the same thing would happen to him. As the slow boat wound its way past the familiar plains and creeks of his youth, Sitting Bull thought of his friend and wondered if he would soon meet him again in the Land of the Spirits.

But when Sitting Bull and his party arrived at Fort Randall the soldiers there greeted him kindly. He was their prisoner, but he was also the most famous Indian in North America and they were all excited to

COURTESY BUFFALO BILL HISTORICAL CENTER, CODY, WYOMING

Sitting Bull after his surrender

see him. In the time he had been away in Canada, his fame had spread so that every schoolchild had heard the story of Sitting Bull and the Battle of the Little Bighorn.

Before long, visitors from all around the country began coming to Fort Randall to see Sitting Bull. Other Indian chiefs came to ask his advice. Newspaper reporters came to interview him. Writers and scholars came to ask questions. Artists came to paint portraits of him. And sometimes people who were just curious came to have a word with "the most notorious Indian alive."

Sitting Bull enjoyed the attention, but, even so, he was unhappy at Fort Randall. He longed to be back with his own people, and once again to be a chief among them. The only thing that gave him the will to continue was the hope that someday he would be allowed to join them at Standing Rock.

Patiently he waited, but for a long time nothing happened. Then, at last, in May 1883, a message came from Washington, D.C. The white chiefs had decided that Sitting Bull could not be held personally responsible for Custer's death. Sitting Bull was free to go to Standing Rock.

Full of hope, Sitting Bull set out for his new home. He had never wanted a reservation, but now he was willing to work within it for the good of his people. During the long journey he was very busy making plans. And with each passing mile his spirits rose.

But when he met James McLaughlin, the head agent at Standing Rock, his hopes for the future were quickly dashed.

James McLaughlin, or "White Hair," as the Hunkpapas called him, was not the worst of the government's Indian agents. He was married to a half-breed Santee Sioux woman, and knew more than most white people about the Indians. Nevertheless, like most agents, he firmly believed that he alone knew what was best for the Indians under him. In his view the Sioux must abandon their old ways and learn to follow "the white man's road." To McLaughlin, a proud and independent-minded chief like Sitting Bull meant nothing but trouble—and the agent had no intention of working with this chief.

When Sitting Bull tried to discuss his people's future, the agent quickly cut him off. "Do you want to know how you can best help your people?" he asked. Sitting Bull did not reply. McLaughlin led him outside to a field where some other Indians were busy working. "Like this." He handed him a hoe and ordered him to get to work.

Silently Sitting Bull did as he was told. After he had been working for about an hour, the agent called him over again. "Is the work too hard for you?" he asked. Sitting Bull shook his head, "No."

McLaughlin took this as a sign that the stubborn old chief had been broken. "Sitting Bull," he wrote his superiors, "is now thoroughly subdued." But McLaughlin had not understood his rival.

Sitting Bull had no objection to hard work. But he was not about to let anyone tell him what to do—not without a fight. Despite everything, he was still a chief. And it was not long before McLaughlin learned this in a very dramatic way.

When Sitting Bull had been at Standing Rock only a few months, a commission of senators arrived from Washington, D.C. They had come to investigate a bill that had been put before the Congress the previous year. This bill gave more than half of the Sioux lands to the United States government. It was the work of two men—Newton Edmunds and Samuel Hinman. Together they had traveled to all the Sioux reservations until they had collected enough Indian signatures to pass the bill. But the Indians claimed that Edmunds and Hinman had lied to them. The two men had not told them that the bill would take away their land. Worse still, they had forced them to sign, telling them that they would be severely punished if they refused. The senators had come to look into these charges, and help the Sioux keep their land.

Sitting Bull, however, knew nothing of this. McLaughlin had carefully kept the meeting and its purpose hidden from him. This was a common practice among reservation agents, who tried to do all they could to break the power of the old Indian chiefs.

When Sitting Bull learned of the meeting, at the last minute, he raced to get there in time. As far as he was concerned, a group of white people meeting with Indians in this way could only mean one thing. They were planning to steal more Indian land.

The meeting had already started when he arrived.

As Sitting Bull had not been told what the meeting was about, he had a hard time understanding what the white people were saying. He did notice one thing, however. They did not want to let him speak. No matter how many times he raised his hand to be called upon, they passed him over. Sitting Bull was a proud man, and he soon ran out of patience. Standing up, he cried, "Do you know who I am?"

The commissioners replied that they knew his name was Sitting Bull. But he was speaking out of turn and had better sit down and be quiet. Sitting Bull then told them that he was chief of the Hunkpapas and they would do well to let him speak. The commissioners again ordered him to sit down and behave himself. At this, Sitting Bull lost his temper. "You have acted like men drinking whiskey," he cried, "and I came here to give you some advice." With that he raised his hand high in the air. Every Indian in the room arose and followed him out the door.

Sitting Bull was glad when he heard the senators murmuring in shocked voices behind him. He had shown those liars and thieves what he thought of them! But then he saw that Gall and the other Hunkpapas looked upset. He asked them what was wrong. Speaking slowly, they said that they were sorry, but he had made a terrible mistake. These white people had not come to steal their land but to help them keep it.

Sitting Bull felt ashamed of himself. He was never sure, he told the others, that any white person could be trusted. But if he had made a mistake, he would apologize for it. That very day he sent a message to the commissioners, saying he would like to meet with them again and apologize.

This second meeting was very crowded, as everyone waited to hear what Sitting Bull would say. As he rose to his feet, a silence fell around the room.

"I am here to apologize for my bad conduct," Sitting Bull began, "and to take back what I said . . . Now I will tell you my mind and I will tell everything straight."

In a strong, clear voice he reviewed the history of his people since the arrival of the white people. He spoke of the treaties broken, the wars, and the betrayals. Now he said he had promised to follow the white people's path and had no intention of breaking that promise. He only asked that he and his people be treated with justice.

His people had been robbed of their way of life. Now they must be given help so that they could learn to live as the white people did. They had never farmed—but now the white people wanted to make them farmers. They had never learned to read or write—but in the white person's world, one must know these things. The white people had taken the Indian's land and killed off the buffalo, which had always supported them. It was only fair, Sitting Bull said, that the white people now help the Indians by giving them tools to farm with, livestock to raise, and an education so that they could support themselves in the white people's way.

Sitting Bull concluded:

"If a man loses anything, and goes back and looks carefully for it, he will find it, and that is what the Indians are doing now when they ask you to give them the things that were promised them in the past, and I do not consider that they should be treated like beasts, and that is the reason I have grown up with the feelings I have . . ."

The commissioners did not accept Sitting Bull's apology in the spirit in which it was offered. Instead they leaped to the attack. They were extremely angry because Sitting Bull had accused them of being drunks! Besides, they had no interest in hearing *his* view of the Indian problem. He was not a chief any longer. Like any other reservation Indian, he was dependent for everything on the "goodwill and kindness" of the United States government. "You have no following," they said, "no power, no control, and no right to any control . . ."

It was more than Sitting Bull could bear. Once again he raised his hand high and, with the other Indians behind him, strode from the room.

The commissioners were angry, but agent James McLaughlin was more than angry.

Sitting Bull had made him look foolish. Now everyone was asking who was the real master at Standing Rock—agent McLaughlin or Sitting Bull? McLaughlin never forgave the chief. From that day on he did all he could to break Sitting Bull completely. Never again did he ask his advice or give him any responsibility. McLaughlin even tried to build up his own chiefs to rival Sitting Bull. One of these was Gall; the other, a young Hunkpapa named John Grass. But no matter what McLaughlin did, Sitting Bull remained as popular with his own people as ever. McLaughlin could not understand it.

"He had no single quality," McLaughlin wrote of Sitting Bull years later, "that would serve to draw his people to him, yet he was by far the most influential man of his nation for many years."

As time passed, McLaughlin grew more and more frustrated. It seemed that there was nothing he could do to get rid of his rival.

In 1885 a visitor arrived at Standing Rock to see agent McLaughlin with a plan that seemed to be the answer to his prayers.

His name was Buffalo Bill Cody, and he wanted Sitting Bull to join his all-new Wild West Show on a tour of fifteen American cities.

McLaughlin was excited by the idea. He only wished that Buffalo Bill would take Sitting Bull off his hands forever.

And so it was that Sitting Bull, who had never before been east of the Missouri River, decided to take a trip across America with Buffalo Bill and his group of sharpshooters and cowboys, dancing girls and rodeo riders.

Like Sitting Bull himself, Buffalo Bill Cody was a legend in his own time. He had long, flowing silver hair, a piercing gaze, and he always wore a spanking-new white buckskin suit. To millions of Americans, he looked like a picture-postcard ideal of the man of the Old West. To them Buffalo Bill symbolized the exciting adventures of cowboys and Indians, vast prairies and open skies. He was a genuine hero of the Old West—a man who stood for a way of life that was rapidly becoming history. But that summer Sitting Bull stole even Buffalo Bill's thunder.

To the crowds who gathered to see "Custer's killer" in the flesh, Sitting Bull was the real man of the West, in a way that even Buffalo Bill could never be. He had lived there long before the land had been "civilized." He had seen the cowboys come, fought in the wars, and lived the life that was already known to most only through colorful songs and stories. To the audiences who were so eager to see him, Sitting Bull was a relic from another time. And perhaps nothing else Sitting Bull had ever seen or done alerted him to how much the world had changed.

Each night he rode out to the crack of gunfire. Then he paraded before hollering crowds. When they saw him, they screamed "Custer's killer," and then lined up by the hundreds to buy a picture that he had written his name on, or simply to shake his hand. It had all become a game.

On this tour Sitting Bull saw for the first time the sights of the white people's world. He visited great stores with glass fronts. He

114

Buffalo Bill Cody

walked down avenues crowded with people and carriages. He saw enormous buildings made of stone, and huge ships of steel. But everything he saw only made him homesick for his own people and their old way of life. In comparison, the world of the Indian seemed so simple, so honest.

The white people had so much. Why, then, were so many of their people poor and hungry? Sitting Bull could not understand why. Among the Indians everything had always been shared equally. But the white people did not seem to care if their people starved to death. Sitting Bull could not live that way. Years later, his costar, the sharpshooter Annie Oakley, remembered that wherever Sitting Bull went while on tour, he was surrounded by ragged little beggar boys. Most of the money he earned went into their pockets. "The white man," he told Annie Oakley,

115

"knows how to make everything, but he does not know how to distribute it."

When the tour was over, Sitting Bull got ready to return to Standing Rock.

Buffalo Bill begged him to sail with the show to Europe, but the old chief refused. He was needed back at the reservation. Once again the white people were talking of taking Sioux land. And so Buffalo Bill bade him farewell. In parting he gave Sitting Bull a big white sombrero hat with an American flag stitched in its band. He also gave the chief an old gray circus horse he had grown fond of. The horse had been trained to kneel down and lift its hoof at the sound of gunfire.

Agent McLaughlin was not happy to see Sitting Bull back at the reservation. For a time, however, life at Standing Rock was quiet, with no sign of any plan to take away the Sioux lands that were left.

In 1888, however, another commission arrived at Standing Rock. This time they had come for more Sioux land. The government wanted to break apart the Great Sioux Reservation into six smaller reservations. This would give the white people nine million more acres of Sioux land.

As soon as Sitting Bull heard this, he went to work. He tried to persuade Gall and John Grass—agent McLaughlin's chiefs—to join him in fighting this swindle. The commission already had been to many reservations and had gotten many Indian signatures, but they could do nothing if the Hunkpapas refused to sign.

The commission was headed by the Hunkpapas' old enemy, General George "Three Stars" Crook. He had beaten them, and they had beaten him many times. But, strangely enough, many of the Hunkpapas had great respect for him. This was because he never lied to them, as the other white people did. This time, however, the truth that General Crook had to tell them was unpleasant indeed. "The white people in the East are like birds," Crook said. "They are hatching out of their eggs every year, and there is not enough room in the East. They must go elsewhere and they come West, as you have seen them coming. And they will come until they overrun all of this country." Crook told the Indians that if they did not agree to lose much of their land now, they were sure to lose it all later.

After Gall and John Grass had listened to what Crook had to say, they were not sure what to do. Perhaps General Crook was right. But

Sitting Bull had no such doubts. If the Sioux agreed this time, it would not be long before the white people came back and asked for still more land. Their only hope was to fight.

He quickly called his people together and spoke of what was happening:

> *"They want us to give up another chunk of our tribal land. This is not the first time nor the last time. They will try to gain possession of the last piece of ground we possess. They are again telling us what they intend to do if we agree to their wishes. Have we ever set a price on our land and received such a value? No. We never did ... They promised us how we are going to live peaceably on the land we still own, how they are going to show us a new way of living. They even promised us how we can go to heaven when we die. But what have we gotten from the promises of the Great White Father? Only this: We are dying off in expectation of getting the things we were promised."*

Sitting Bull spoke like a hopeless old man, but many of the Hunkpapas heard in his words the lost pride and fire of their nation. They lined up behind him. They would not sign away the last bits of their nation.

But Sitting Bull's enemy, agent McLaughlin, was working just as hard to make sure the Hunkpapas voted Yes. It was a personal fight for him now, and he was determined to beat Sitting Bull any way he could.

In the dead of night McLaughlin arranged a secret meeting with John Grass, the young chief. He gave him a speech he had written himself. He put pressure on the young man to change his position and convince the other Hunkpapas that the commission was right. Grass was unsure of himself. He agreed. Then McLaughlin went to work on Gall. He spoke to him at every opportunity and did all he could to scare Gall so that he would support the commission. He assured him that giving in to the commission's demands was the Hunkpapas' only hope. Gall was an honorable man, but he was a fighter—a warrior, not a thinker. A man of few words, he was not able to resist the agent's arguments. He, too, said he would work for the new agreement.

As soon as McLaughlin was sure of the support of these two men, and their followers, he hastily called a final meeting of the commission for August 3, 1888. Gall and John Grass were ordered to be there. But Sitting Bull and his followers deliberately were told nothing.

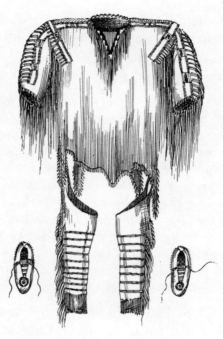

Sioux dress and moccasins

As soon as Sitting Bull learned that the commission was meeting, he rushed to get there. But he arrived too late. Gall, John Grass, and the Hunkpapas with them had all signed the agreement. The Great Sioux Reservation was a thing of the past.

Sitting Bull felt old and worn out. He turned to leave the council grounds, but before he could get away, a newspaper reporter grabbed him by the arm. "Sitting Bull?" the reporter asked eagerly. "How do the Indians feel about giving up nine million acres of their land?"

Sitting Bull turned on him, his eyes blazing.

"Indians!" he cried in the language of his fathers. "There are no Indians left but me."

118

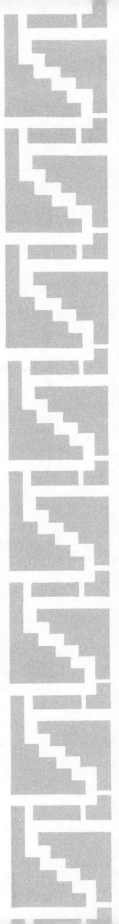

ꙮꙮꙮꙮꙮ **16** ꙮꙮꙮꙮꙮ

The Dance of Ghosts

It was a dark time for Sitting Bull.

He retreated to the log cabin he had built in a distant corner of the reservation. There he occupied himself with planting a garden and taking care of his two wives and many children and grandchildren. He began planting crops, but the weather was bad that year and he soon gave it up. His heart was not in it anyway. He did not want to follow the white people's road any longer. Often he passed his days dreaming of old times, when he had been young and strong-hearted, and the Great Spirit Wakan Tanka had spoken in his ear. The old ways were being abandoned now. Even the spirits seemed to have fallen silent. And so, as always, Sitting Bull wrote himself a song:

> *"A warrior I have been*
> *Now*
> *It is all over*
> *A hard time I have."*

By 1889 hard times were widespread for the Sioux. First there was no rain and the crops failed. Soon there was a drought, and on all the reservations people were going hungry. With hunger came white people's diseases. Measles, whooping cough, and influenza struck one after the other, killing the Sioux in great numbers. It did not take much, after all, to snuff out the life of a starving child or an old man without enough clothes to stay warm. For all the white people's talk of education and progress, their way was only leading the Sioux to poverty and death.

Sitting Bull and the Hunkpapas were growing desperate.

Then, in October 1890, a Miniconjou named Kicking Bear came to Standing Rock to see Sitting Bull. Kicking Bear told the old chief a strange and wonderful story.

He said that he and his friends had traveled far away to the place where the sun sets. There they had met a Paiute Indian named Wovoka. Wovoka was no ordinary Indian but a new human form of the savior who had come to earth once before. The savior had left that time because the white people had treated him so badly. But now he had returned, this time in the body of an Indian.

Wovoka told Kicking Bear and the others that he had come to teach them a magic dance, which he called the Dance of the Ghosts. If the Indians danced this dance, they would bring their dead ancestors back to life, and they would be able to see and speak with loved ones they had lost. This dance also would prepare the way for Wovoka to come and save them.

Next spring, Wovoka told them, he would send a great rain of earth down upon the world. All the white people would be buried beneath it. The Indians who believed in him would be saved, however, for he would lift them up into the sky with him. Only when all the earth had fallen, and all traces of the old world had been wiped out, would they be brought back down again. The world these Indians would enter would be new and golden. There they would find all their dead brought back to life again. The buffalo and other game would once more roam the plains in great numbers, and the land would be untouched and unscarred. In this new world the Indians would live in peace and happiness forever.

Kicking Bear then told Sitting Bull that he and his friends had been taught how to dance this ghost dance. On their way back home, the

Miniconjous had danced it in the middle of an empty plain. Afterwards, they had come upon a camp filled with their dead friends and relatives, to whom they had spoken. They also had come across a herd of buffalo, even though everyone knew all the buffalo were dead. Kicking Bear had killed one of these buffalo with his bow and arrows. Then he and his friends had roasted and eaten it. But when they were done, they saw the bones put themselves back together. And then, to their amazement, they watched as a new living buffalo rose out of the skeleton of the old.

For a long time Kicking Bear continued to describe this experience. He had come, he said, to teach Sitting Bull and his people how to perform the ghost dance so that they, too, might be saved.

Sitting Bull was not convinced. Kicking Bear's story sounded too wonderful to be true. He had seen much magic in his time. Still he did not think it was possible for the dead to come back to life. But the other Hunkpapas who were listening to the story begged Sitting Bull to let Kicking Bear stay and teach them the magic dance. It would be a terrible thing if they were the only Indians left behind when Wovoka came to take all who believed in him to a new and better world.

Sitting Bull yielded to their pleas. He invited Kicking Bear to stay as his guest. Within days the reservation was full of ghost dancing.

Standing Rock was not the only place where the Dance of the Ghosts was being practiced. Ghost dancing was sweeping across all the Sioux reservations. The great Red Cloud had become a convert, and so had Sioux everywhere. In Pine Ridge, Rosebud, Grand River, and Cheyenne River, the Indians were dancing.

As Wovoka had preached, the ghost dancers wore special "ghost shirts." These were painted all over in white with magic symbols of stars,

A Sioux dance mirror

121

moons, eagles, and buffalo. Wovoka said that these shirts would make the dancers bulletproof, and protect them from anyone who tried to hurt them. Despite the shirts, however, the Indians themselves were not to fight the white people. Nor were they to fight back if attacked. They were only to dance peacefully, to love their brothers, and to wait for the day when their savior would come.

By the end of October so many Indians were ghost dancing that all other activities had been abandoned. Fields were left unplanted. Schools were empty as young and old began to dance. Soon the only sounds that could be heard on all the Sioux reservations were the low chants and shuffling feet of the ghost dancers.

The agents who headed the reservations grew frightened. So did the settlers whose ranches and stores now dotted the once empty landscape. What were the Indians planning now? Would they try to make war on them again? What was the meaning of the Dance of the Ghosts? Some even began to wonder if perhaps the Indians did have some magic power—a magic power that would hurt them. These white people did not care that the ghost dance was basically Christian. It looked like a strange new religion to them, and they were terrified. They wanted it stopped.

But day by day the craze grew. More and more Indians joined in the dance. They had lost so much—their land, their means of support. The very fabric of their lives had been destroyed. Now they seized on the ghost dance as something that would give them hope. Everywhere new ghost-dancing songs were written and sung, expressing their fears and their desires. Often these songs were cries for help to the Great Spirit who had been silent for so long:

> *"My father have pity on me!*
> *I have nothing to eat*
> *I am dying of thirst*
> *Everything is gone."*

Many reservation agents understood that the ghost-dance religion came out of the desperation of the Indians. These agents believed the best way to take care of the problem was to wait. In time the movement would surely fade away of its own accord. McLaughlin at Standing Rock was one of those who felt this way. But then the agent at the nearby Pine

Ridge Reservation gave in to panic, and suddenly the Dance of the Ghosts became a crisis.

Mr. D.F. Royer, the Pine Ridge agent, was young and did not have much experience. A nervous, timid man, he did not feel at ease with the Indians at the best of times. In fact his feelings were so obvious that the Pine Ridge Indians had nicknamed him Young-Man-Afraid-of-the-Sioux. They had laughed at him for being so afraid, but now his fear was to cause them much hardship. For by mid-November all the Indians at Pine Ridge were dancing, and nothing could convince agent Royer they would not soon start fighting. "Indians are dancing in the snow and are wild and crazy!" he telegraphed Washington, D.C. "We need protection and we need it now. We need at least a thousand soldiers, maybe more . . ."

Washington responded quickly. Soldiers were sent marching. All the reservation agents were asked to send immediately the names of every Indian behind the disturbing new religion.

Agent McLaughlin at Standing Rock did not hesitate. There was no evidence to prove him right. But he was convinced that Sitting Bull, and Sitting Bull alone, was responsible. His name was at the head of McLaughlin's list.

The name Sitting Bull was all the generals in Washington, D.C., needed to see. The old chief was up to his old tricks. They must put a stop to him. Then they could take care of the others.

From U.S. Army headquarters in Chicago, orders for Sitting Bull's arrest were sent out. To avoid trouble, the generals chose Buffalo Bill Cody to do the job. He was one of the few white people with whom Sitting Bull was friendly. He, if anyone, could persuade Sitting Bull to come in without a fight.

Buffalo Bill immediately set out for Standing Rock.

He felt bad at having to arrest the "Chief," as he called him. But he knew that if he did not do it, someone else would. And he had an idea that agent McLaughlin's men would be only too happy to make things as difficult as possible for his old friend. Buffalo Bill planned to make the arrest as smooth as he could.

When he arrived at Standing Rock, however, he discovered that his orders had been recalled. McLaughlin was determined to take charge of this arrest all by himself. Sitting Bull belonged to him, and no one else.

He made it clear that he did not want any "show business outsiders" interfering.

And so Buffalo Bill was sent on his way.

Long into the night, McLaughlin thought about what would be the best way to arrest his old enemy. He did not want any trouble—especially from the other Indians. At last he hit upon a plan. He would use Indian policemen to arrest the chief. When Sitting Bull saw that he was being given over by his own people, surely he would go quietly.

From his small log cabin, Sitting Bull could feel the net tightening around him. Everyone knew that big trouble was coming because of the ghost dance. Soldiers were marching, and now people were coming to him, whispering that he was soon to be placed under arrest. On December 14 he heard that Buffalo Bill Cody had arrived at Standing Rock. Buffalo Bill had come, people warned Sitting Bull, to take him away. Then Sitting Bull was told that Buffalo Bill had gone away again. That meant that policemen and soldiers would be coming instead.

On December 15 many visitors came to Sitting Bull's small cabin. Crowds of young men arrived, many of them ghost dancers. They said that they had come to protect him and stop any arrests from being made. Among these young men were Sitting Bull's nephew, Jumping Bull; a fine young warrior named Catch-the-Bear; and Brave Thunder and Strikes-the-Kettle, all strong, determined men. When night fell they gathered in a tight cluster around the isolated cabin.

It was a bitterly cold night with much wind and snow. But this did not bother the young men. They had made up their minds to guard Sitting Bull, and were prepared to stay outside, all night if necessary. Hours passed. The moon rose, shining with a clear light over the silent world. The young men remained awake, watching. The moon set in the sky, and the first rays of sun appeared faint in the distance, until everything around looked as pale as the land of ghosts. The first birds began to sing, and slowly the young men began to fall asleep. It did not look as if the policemen were coming.

Inside the cabin, Sitting Bull fell into a deep, dreamless sleep. He was awakened abruptly.

A large man was shaking him, pulling him roughly from the bed. Through eyes thick with sleep, Sitting Bull recognized him. His name was Lieutenant Bull Head, a large, slow-moving Hunkpapa who was one of White Hair McLaughlin's favorites.

Sitting Bull

"What do you want here?" cried Sitting Bull, still only half-awake.

"You are my prisoner now!" Bull Head replied. "You must come to the agency."

Sitting Bull sat up slowly. "Let me put on my clothes," he said mildly. "Then I'll come with you."

Outside the cabin there was a noise of stamping feet, pushing and shoving. More policemen came through the door. Sitting Bull knew them all—Red Tomahawk, Gray Eagle. He had known them as boys, and had proudly watched them grow up into young men. Now they had come to arrest him.

His two wives were awake by this time. Proud women, they shouted scornfully at the policemen who had come to take their husband away. Lieutenant Bull Head was growing nervous. A large crowd of Sitting Bull's friends and relatives had gathered outside. They were in an ugly mood, ready for a fight. "Hurry!" cried Bull Head, prodding at Sitting Bull with his gun. At his orders the forty-three policemen who agent McLaughlin had sent to arrest Sitting Bull circled the cabin. Then Bull Head and Red Tomahawk seized the chief, still only half-dressed, and pushed him out of the cabin.

Sitting Bull did not show any fear, but he did not protest either. He felt too sick in his heart to fight. Whatever happened would happen.

Outside the cabin, however, the crowd had grown to almost a hundred. They stood shouting curses at Bull Head and his men. Among them was Sitting Bull's seventeen-year-old son, Crow Foot. A brave boy, he rushed up to his father, and pushing at the policemen, cried out: "You can't take him! You won't take him." Sitting Bull tried to quiet him, but the boy would not listen. Then, from a distance, Sitting Bull heard one of his wives sing:

> *Sitting Bull, you have always been a brave man*
> *What is going to happen now?*

Sitting Bull felt as if his heart would break. He looked at the friends and relatives who had come to help him. He looked at the policemen, men of his own people, whom the white people had persuaded to betray him. "No!" he cried. "I am not going. Get away! Get away!" And he struggled against the men who held him.

Catch-the-Bear stood nearby. He had been waiting for this moment. Now he pulled a rifle from beneath the blanket he wore around him. "You shall not take him," he cried, and fired his gun, straight at Lieutenant Bull Head.

Bull Head fell, dying. As he did, he took aim at Catch-the-Bear. But Bull Head was fading, and the bullet hit Sitting Bull instead. Red Tomahawk then fired in a panic. His bullet too went straight into Sitting Bull. As the shots rang out, the old gray circus horse, trained to the sound of gunfire, began to kneel and lift its hoof over and over again. And so Sitting Bull, great chief of the Hunkpapas, breathed his last. He was fifty-six years old.

When his friends and relatives realized what had happened, they began to wail and sob—a sharp sound piercing the clear morning air. Hot-headed young men pulled out their guns and began to fire. The policemen fought back, and the battle continued until McLaughlin sent in troops to beat down Sitting Bull's supporters.

When the fight was over, six policemen were dead, as were eight of Sitting Bull's friends and relatives, among them his seventeen-year-old son Crow Foot.

Sitting Bull's long fight for his nation was over.

Epilogue

News of Sitting Bull's death soon spread from reservation to reservation, and there was sorrow everywhere. Perhaps if the Sioux had not still believed in the ghost dance, they would have risen up against the white people in memory of their hero. But as it was, they only danced. As they danced they prayed for the day when their savior would come and their world would be given back to them.

After Sitting Bull was killed, many of the Hunkpapas felt a sense of panic and fled by the hundreds to other reservations. But things were bad all over. It was said that the soldiers were coming to stop the ghost dance forever, and all the Sioux were afraid.

Some of the Hunkpapas joined the camp of Chief Big Foot of the Miniconjou. His people were camped on Cherry Creek by the Cheyenne River Agency. But when Big Foot learned of Sitting Bull's death, he decided to move his camp to the Pine Ridge Agency. Pine Ridge, under Oglala Chief

Red Cloud, was the largest Sioux Reservation left. There, Big Foot believed, his people would be safe even if the soldiers came.

On December 27 Big Foot's camp set out through the freezing countryside. They traveled as fast as they could, but Chief Big Foot was an old man, and he was sick with pneumonia. Soon he began to cough up blood, and the others slowed down to keep him from getting any sicker. But they were scared. Soldiers were everywhere, and it was not safe for any Indian outside the reservations.

The very next day the soldiers found them.

Four troops of the Seventh Cavalry—the same regiment that had fought under General Custer at the Little Bighorn—came riding over the hills. When they saw Big Foot's band, they drew their guns. Their leader, Major Samuel Whitside, then informed Chief Big Foot that he had orders to treat any Indians found outside the reservations as hostile. Big Foot and his people must come with him and his soldiers to the Seventh Cavalry camp at Wounded Knee Creek. There they would be forced to turn over all their weapons and horses.

Big Foot was too tired and sick to protest. He ordered his people to do as the soldiers said. Slowly the camp of one hundred and twenty men and two hundred and thirty women and children began to march over the hills to the frozen creek where the great warrior Crazy Horse was said to be buried. By the time they reached the ice-covered banks of Wounded Knee, dusk had fallen.

Major Whitside ordered them to make camp by the banks of the creek. In the morning he and his men would take their guns and horses. Then he promised he would escort them to Pine Ridge.

Big Foot and his people did as they were told. By tomorrow night they would all be safe.

But after dark, Colonel James Forsyth, commander of the Seventh Cavalry, rode up to the camp with the rest of his soldiers. He told Major Whitside that he would now take charge of Big Foot and his people. Big Foot's band, he said, was deeply involved in the ghost dance. He had orders not to take them to Pine Ridge, but to escort them one and all to the newly built Union Pacific Railroad. There they would be taken to military prison in Omaha.

As the moon rose, and the stars shone icily, Forsyth and the Seventh Cavalry settled down to wait for morning. They passed the time playing cards and drinking whiskey in the shadow of Big Foot's make-shift camp. By morning many of them were drunk and in a nasty mood.

Roughly they awoke Big Foot and his people and ordered them to hand over all their weapons immediately. Most did as they were asked. But the soldiers were still not satisfied. They went from tepee to tepee, ripping apart blankets, tearing up sacks of provisions, and destroying as much as they could. They added the few weapons they found—mostly hunting knives—to the large pile in the center of the camp. Then, not convinced they had found all the Indians' weapons, they began to search the bodies of Big Foot's braves.

Many of these men were wearing their magic ghost shirts. They were afraid that if they took them off, the soldiers would shoot them. They tried to refuse, but the soldiers ran up and began to tear the shirts from their backs. At this an angry murmur rose from the crowd. A medicine man by the name of Yellow-Bird began to shuffle slowly back and forth in the steps of the ghost dance. And, almost under his breath, he began to sing a ghost-dance song. "They will not hurt you," he sang. "The bullets will not go through," he continued, referring to Wovoka's promise that the magic shirts would protect the Indians from any harm, no matter what the soldiers did. Soon more people began to sing.

The mood was tense, but so far nothing had happened.

Suddenly the soldiers began to shout in loud, angry voices.

One of the Indians, a young Miniconjou named Black Coyote, had a rifle! Rushing toward him, the soldiers shouted that he must give it to them at once. Black Coyote lifted the rifle high over his head. It had cost him very much money, he cried. It was his and he did not want to give it to the soldiers. The soldiers drew closer. One of them pushed Black Coyote as hard as he could, making him spin around until he was dizzy. Black Coyote lifted his precious rifle higher. Again the soldier pushed at him. Suddenly the gun went off. Later many of the Indians said it was surely an accident. Black Coyote knew better than to fire at the soldiers. When the smoke had cleared, one of the soldiers lay on the ground, dead. When the other soldiers saw him, they all lifted their guns and began to fire as fast as they could at the unarmed Indians. "They shot at us," said one woman later, "like we were buffalo." Some of Big Foot's braves tried to get back their weapons and fight, but the soldiers far outnumbered them, and they could do nothing.

No one ever knew exactly how many Indians died that day on the banks of Wounded Knee Creek. Many believe it was close to three hundred, most of them women and children. Chief Big Foot also was killed. As for the soldiers, who had gone crazy with their guns, they lost twenty-five—most to their own bullets.

The Indians who were still alive were loaded up into a wooden wagon and carried to the Pine Ridge Agency. That night a blizzard came, and snow fell across the land, covering the banks of Wounded Knee Creek. The dead were left on the frozen ground by the creek until New Year's Day, 1891, when they were buried by a detachment of soldiers in a mass, unmarked grave.

The white people had done all they could to destroy the proud Sioux nation.

The ghost dance had not saved the Indians of Chief Big Foot. The magic shirts had not held back the white people's bullets. Nor, the Sioux now saw, would their savior ever come. Wounded Knee was the grave-yard of their hopes. As a boy the Oglala medicine man Black Elk had known both Sitting Bull and Crazy Horse. And he had seen both the Battle of the Little Bighorn and the massacre at Wounded Knee. He said:

> *"When I look down now from this high hill of my old age, I can still see the butchered women and children lying heaped and scattered all along the crooked gulch as plain as when I saw them with eyes still young. And I can see that something else died there in the bloody mud, and was buried in the blizzard. A people's dream died there. It was a beautiful dream . . . "*

Far off, in Standing Rock, North Dakota, was the man who had dreamed this dream more strongly than any other. He lay buried in a plain pine wooden box on the slope of a hill facing the sunset. On his grave was the simple marker: Sitting Bull, died Dec. 15, 1890.

Suggested Reading

Anderson, LaVere. *Sitting Bull: Great Sioux Chief.* Champaign, IL: Garrard Publishing Company, 1972.

Bleeker, Sonia. *Sioux Indians:Hunters and Warriors of the Plains.* New York: William Morrow & Company, 1962.

Brown, Dee. *Bury My Heart at Wounded Knee: An Indian History of the American West.* New York: Holt, Rinehart & Winston, 1974.

Freedman, Russell. *Indian Chiefs.* New York: Holiday House, 1987.

Garst, Shannon. *Sitting Bull: Champion of his People.* New York: Julian Messner, Inc., 1946.

Josephy, Alvin M., Jr. *The Patriot Chiefs.* New York: Viking Press, 1961.

Stevenson, Augusta. *Sitting Bull: Dakota Boy.* Indianapolis, IN: Bobbs-Merrill Company, Inc., 1960.

Vestal, Stanley. *Sitting Bull, Champion of the Sioux.* Norman, OK: University of Oklahoma Press, 1957.